D0575280

The Big Book
of Afghans

The Big Book of Afghans

Annette Feldman

Designed by Allan Mogel
Photography by Ernest Silva

A Genie Book

VNR VAN NOSTRAND REINHOLD COMPANY
New York Cincinnati Toronto London Melbourne

Copyright © 1981 by Genie Books
Library of Congress Catalog Card Number 81-7524
ISBN: 0-442-22528-8

All rights reserved. No part of this work covered by the
copyright hereon may be reproduced or used in any form or
by any means—graphic, electronic, or mechanical, including
photocopying, recording, taping, or information storage and
retrieval systems—without written permission of the publisher.

Printed in the United States of America
Prepared and produced by Genie Books, New York, New York

Published by Van Nostrand Reinhold Company
  135 West 50th Street
    New York, 10020

Van Nostrand Reinhold Limited
1410 Birchmount Road
Scarborough, Ontario M1P 2E7, Canada

Van Nostrand Reinhold Australia Pty. Ltd.
17 Queen Street
Mitcham, Victoria 3132, Australia

Van Nostrand Reinhold Company Limited
Molly Millars Lane
Wokingham, Berkshire, England

16   15   14   13   12   11   10   9   8   7   6   5   4   3   2   1

Library of Congress Cataloging in Publication Data

Feldman, Annette.
  The big book of afghans.

  "A Genie book."
  Includes index.
  1. Afghans (Coverlets)   I. Title
TT825.F44   746.9′7′041   81-7524
ISBN 0-442-22528-8   AACR2

Dedicated to

The Memory of My Parents
Gertrude and Emanuel Gerber

and to
Irving Feldman, My Husband
Valerie Kurita, My Assistant and Close Associate
Dena Kuttner and Claire Borham, Special Friends

and
"My Hands" Without Whom This Book
Would Not Have Been Possible:
Antonia Builes, Marjorie Williams,
Rita Quinn, and Bertha Zeltser

Contents

/ Crocheted Lap Robes

/ Crocheted Crib Blankets

Introduction

Afghans are big and beautiful and, perhaps, one of the most reassuring, comforting things on earth to throw over your knees or toss around your shoulders to stave off the chilly rawness of the middle seasons. If you already count an afghan among your treasures, it was probably one passed on to you by a cherished grandma or dear old aunt who lived long ago and far away; today, it is probably a lovely reminder to have of that person's tender loving hands, one made even more special considering the difficulty in days past with just securing such a thing as yarn. Money was scarce, little yarn was available, and what there was of it was more often than not the bits and pieces resulting from the unraveling of worn-out woolen clothing and blankets.

Cherish your heirlooms, but know also that the wheels of progress have put you in a position today where you can easily make your own afghans, for your use now and, later, to be passed along as keepsakes for future generations. Yarns are readily available—in the complete spectrum of colors—so that it is no longer necessary to "recycle"; needles and hooks have been sizing gradually upward for the past few decades so that you don't have to struggle with the sliver-thin needles used exclusively in years past; and patterns abound for both knitted and crocheted pieces.

An interesting note: As familiar as the word *afghan* is to all of us, there is, oddly enough, no dictionary defining it as the warm, luxurious, blanketlike covering we know it as. My own thoughts are that somewhere along the way, the word became associated with the natives of Afghanistan, whose custom it was, and still is, to make small colorful, woolen rugs, similar in concept and design to the kinds of afghans we think about, for a variety of purposes.

Whether this be true or not, my intent in writing this book is to encourage you to make as many afghans as you are able to or want to, in the easiest way possible. The thirty-six afghans appearing here I have designed with the knowledge of the colorful yarns and larger needles and hooks available today. Each is a composition especially worked out to make your handcrafting as easy and pleasurable as possible. Large as the finished projects are, all of them are made up of "carry-along" pieces that can comfortably be taken along with you to be worked on anywhere at any time the mood strikes you. All

8

the pieces are worked separately into geometric shapes—squares, ovals, rectangles, triangles—and then joined, almost jigsaw-fashion, into a whole and finished with an appropriate edging or fringing.

Among the patterns, most are multicolored except for those few in which the stitch itself is so interesting that it should take precedence over color. Some of the afghans are quite contemporary in design, whereas others are very traditional. In between is a whole range of patterns eclectic enough to be attractive in any setting. Among the crib blankets, woolly lambs wander about on one, while tiny appliquéd bows and a delicate, variegated lace edges another. In the lap-robe group is a warm, "furry" knitted piece rugged enough even an ex-quarterback would feel comfortable pulling it over his knees at a late-autumn football game, as well as one crocheted of linked "daisy" chains, great as a wrap-up for long drives or as a gift for someone confined to a wheelchair. As for the full-size afghans, you need only thumb through the pages to see which and how many you want to make—or make first. Among them are the Garden of Roses, in which a textured black background is sprinkled with pink and crimson roses; Windswept, on which delicate, long-stemmed flowers sway across a pale yellow background; and Granny Goes Free-Form, perhaps the most unusual version of the simple granny-square afghan to be found anywhere.

Clear, easy-to-follow directions have been written for the making of these afghans. Most of the knit and crochet stitches that have been drawn on are simple ones, easy enough for even the novice to follow, particularly with the help of the "how-to" Stitch Glossary at the back of the book (p.147). For those of you who would like to alter the patterns, perhaps enlarging a lap robe to full size, or change the color scheme, you should encounter no problem because all the projects have been made of small pieces that can be made shorter, narrower, longer or wider. These designs, properly hung or padded and lined, can also be made into dramatic wall hangings or area rugs.

It has been fun for me to design this book for you. It is now my desire that you have as much fun in making the projects in it and that you derive the full, long-term pleasure that comes from having created something beautiful.

Be Proud of Your Finished Handwork

The pleasure you take in doing any piece of handwork should be equaled, if not surpassed, by the enjoyment you will derive from it when you've finished. You can easily make this the case—as well as have your work as nearly perfect as is necessary to make you proud of it—by expending a little extra effort. Careful attention to a few, simple, relatively painless working rules will prove to give you good results, regardless of what you have made, particularly if it is something as large and important as one of the afghans from this book. Some of these guidelines are of a general nature, applying to good work habits in any handcraft endeavor, whereas others refer to the specific working of projects involving the making and assembling of small pieces into a whole. I've tried to set them down simply and to offer whatever helpful advice I can towards making you happy with what you've made.

As you work, remember that because needlework involves no more than the use of your own two hands, some yarn, and a hook or pair of needles, it is one of the most creative of the crafts, one that puts you in the forefront as the creator of a piece of fabric ultimately destined to be turned into something lovely to wear or use in your home.

Your Yarn

First things first, you will need yarn before getting started on whatever it is you are about to make. Be careful in your selection of this: What you buy should be of a quality good enough to warrant the amount of time and effort you will be putting into your work. A few extra pennies spent in this direction will be well worth the price if you are assured that, among other things, the yarn is color-fast and of a texture and ply that won't ravel or fray. Having made your choice, be sure that you buy enough of it to finish your project, since dye lots do vary. Though there might be only a small variation of color between the lots, it could be enough to spoil the look of your finished work. Yarn shopkeepers are usually very cooperative in helping you resolve this problem by either putting extra skeins "on hold" for you or gladly refunding the price of leftover skeins.

Your Needles or Hook

Needle or hook size for each project is given along with the instructions for each afghan. These sizes, however, are the ones *we* used in each instance to produce a certain finished measurement with the yarn specified. The tension of each pair of working hands will vary enough that you must make your own individual test. In both knitting and crocheting, the term *tension* applies to the number of stitches you work to the inch with the needles or hook and material you are using. The technical word for this particular measurement is *gauge*, perhaps the most important word in either of these crafts. If your gauge is different from that specified in the instructions, your work will be of the wrong size, which will be particularly disastrous when pieces are to be joined. If your work nets more stitches per inch than your instructions call for, the result will be too small; if less, your piece will be too large. To ensure accuracy, work a 4-inch swatch with the needles and yarn you're planning to use. If your sample matches the specified gauge, you're ready to go on with your work; if it doesn't, change the size of your "tools," switching to a smaller hook or set of needles for a swatch that has come out too large or to larger ones if it has come out too small.

The YOU in Your Work

Now that you have yarn and hook or needles in hand, the next consideration, certainly as important as the two preceding ones, comes into play. That is the state of the YOU that you are about to put into your work. For it to have a smooth, even look, you must be relaxed. Tension and nervousness does, unfortunately, reflect itself in handwork. If you feel this kind of tightness, remember that if your work is to be one of pleasure, you must let it be so. Approach it as something you're really going to enjoy doing, hopefully settled—after work or just the normal routine chores of the day—in the most comfortable niche of your home. Have near you whatever working equipment you might need—scissors, tape measure, maybe a yarn needle and stitch holder—and make sure that your niche is well lighted. Then, know the instructions thoroughly. With this set, you will be able to relax to the steady rhythm of your needles or hook or, perhaps, along with the sounds of the radio or TV or in the company of friends and family. If you are at ease, the work you produce will be even, the quality that sets good work apart from mediocre. If, along the way, you make a mistake, don't be angry at yourself or try to wish it away, thinking that maybe it won't show when the piece is finished. Instead, coolly rip the error back to wherever it happened. Once you have corrected it, you will have freed yourself from any anxiety about it and be relaxed enough to continue productively.

Special Hints for Making and Assembling Afghans

Practically all knitted or crocheted pieces must be put together and finished. This is particularly true with large items, such as an afghan, even if it is only of crib or lap-robe size, where you're working with a number of small pieces to be joined into a larger one. Though the type of finishing we refer to is fairly simple, it does need to be done carefully because the final putting together of your piece is as important as the making of the individual parts. Guidelines follow, as well as suggestions toward developing a system for making the smaller pieces.

Making Your "Components"

To make it easier for yourself in the working of "carry-along" pieces, try making all those of one size and shape at the same time. Before you go on to the next "component," complete all the shapes of one color, regardless of size, before going on to another—once you've gotten started with one of a group of pieces, the rest of that group will usually go faster. If, however, you're the kind of person who gets bored with the "sameness," it is no problem to switch from one to another.

Enlarging a Pattern

A few of our afghans call for the enlarging of a pattern to be embroidered over the finished work. In such instances, you will find a grid overlaying the pattern that has been scaled to the proper size. To enlarge the pattern, mark out on a large piece of paper the finished size of the piece according to the chart, divide it into the number of squares appearing on the grid, and then, square by square, copy the pattern onto the new grid. Finally, transfer the pattern to the piece to be embroidered according to the instructions with the pattern.

Changing Yarn Colors

In working out multicolored projects, it is often necessary to change colors in the middle of a row. In knitting, this change is made by simply working the last stitch with the first color and starting the next one with the new. Wherever the change occurs, the new color should be brought around from under the color just dropped so that the yarn will be twisted together and the work lie smooth and flat. The dropped color should be carried loosely across the back so that it does not pucker the stitches. In crochet work, all changes of color are made by working the last stitch of the original color with that color until two loops of that last stitch remain on the hook; then those two loops are removed with the new color.

Working Crocheted Edges around Knitted Pieces

An edging is often crocheted around a finished piece to give it a firmer finish and make it easier to join one piece to another. Since instructions for the colors to be used for this edging are always included with the project, your only other concerns are to work the same number of stitches along each side of the piece so that your work lies flat and to work three stitches in each corner stitch or point (as in a hexagon) as you pass.

Blocking

Anything knitted or crocheted should be blocked, usually with a warm iron run over a damp cloth. Special care should be taken during this step to keep the iron in motion so that an impression of it won't be left on the piece being blocked. In finishing any piece consisting of a number of smaller pieces, it is best to block all the pieces before attempting to put them together to be sure that they are all of the same size. Pieces that are difficult to block, such as those worked on the bias or in hexagon shapes, should be carefully shaped with rust-proof pins on a board. A soaking wet cloth should then be laid over them, after which they should be allowed to dry completely while pinned.

Seaming

Although there are several ways to join needleworked pieces by sewing, the best way to ensure invisible seams is by means of overcasting or making running back stitches (see Stitch Glossary) on the wrong side of the work, taking special care to match stitch for stitch so that the seams lie perfectly flat.

Metric Conversion Table

Linear Measure

1 inch = 2.54 centimeters
12 inches = 1 foot = 0.3048 meter
3 feet = 1 yard = 0.9144 meter

Square Measure

1 square inch = 6.452 square centimeters
144 square inches = 1 square foot = 929.03 square
    centimeters
9 square feet = 1 square yard = 0.8361 square meter

ABBREVIATIONS

beg	beginning
CC	contrast color
ch	chain
dc	double crochet
dec	decrease
dp	double point
hdc	half-double crochet
hk	hook
inc	increase
k	knit
lp(s)	loop(s)
MC	main color
p	purl
pat	pattern
psso	pass slip stitch over
rep	repeat
rnd	round
sc	single crochet
sl st	slip stitch
sp(s)	space(s)
st(s)	stitch(es)
trc	treble crochet
yo	yarn over

Knitted Afghans

1
Shadow
and
Substance

Approximate finished size:
52 by 64 inches

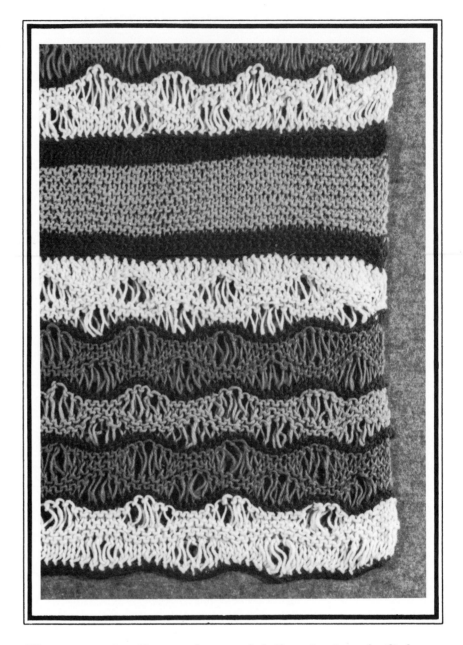

Three repeat patterns of an undulating, textured stitch are knitted in ombré shades of lime, grass, and forest green, each hue outlined with a deep bottle green. Seven strips make up the entire piece.

Materials:
Knitting worsted:
   8 ounces in lime green (A)
   8 ounces in grass green (B)
   8 ounces in forest green (C)
   8 ounces in bottle green (D)
Straight knitting needles, No. 11
Aluminum crochet hook, Size I
Yarn-embroidery needle

Pattern Stitch:
Row 1: K 2, *k 1, yo, k 1, yo twice, k 1, yo three times, k 1, yo twice, k 1, yo, k 5, and rep from * across the row.
Rows 2 and 6: K, dropping all the yo's of the previous row.
Rows 3, 4, 7, and 8: K.
Row 5: K 2, *k 6, yo, k 1, yo twice, k 1, yo three times, k 1, yo twice, k 1, yo, and rep from * across the row to the last 10 sts. End with k 6, yo, k 1, yo twice, k 1, yo three times, k 1, yo twice, k 1.

Repeat Rows 1 through 8 for pattern.

Gauge: 11 stitches = 4 inches in garter st (k every row)

Narrow Strips: Make three: With color D, cast on 142 sts. Working in garter st throughout, work for 2 rows. Change to color C and work 18 rows. Work 2 more rows with color D and bind off loosely.

Wide Strips: Make four: With color A, cast on 142 sts and work Rows 1 through 6. *Change to color D and work Rows 7 and 8. Then change to color B and work Rows 1 through 6. Rep from * three times, substituting C for B on the first repeat and A for B on the third. Bind off.

Finishing: With color D, sl st along the cast-on edge of each narrow strip, working through both lps of each st; fasten off. Then with D, work 1 row along the bound-off edge of each wide strip as follows: With A, work 1 trc in each k st over each plain k st, 1 dc in each k st over the single yo, 1 hdc in each k st over the 2 yo, and 1 sc in each k st over the 3 yo; fasten off. Arrange the strips so that two of the wide strips, cast-on edges to the outside, are at the top and bottom. Alternate narrow strips with the remaining wide between the top and bottom strips, placing the crocheted edges of the wide strips next to the center narrow strip. Join on the wrong side with an overcast st in color D yarn. Finally, with color D, work 1 row of sc along the top and bottom edges of the afghan. Block the piece carefully.

2
An
Irish-Knit
Afghan

Approximate finished size:
  48 by 60 inches excluding fringe

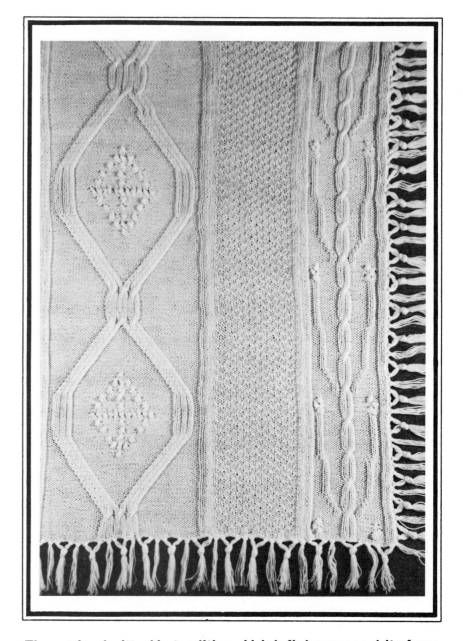

Five strips knitted in traditional Irish fisherman white form this afghan. The main pieces are worked in double-seed, stockinette, and reverse stockinette stitches, interspersed with interesting cables and bobbles, and then joined. Finally, the completed piece is edged with an unusual fringe.

Materials:
Knitting worsted:
    64 ounces in fisherman white
Straight knitting needles, No. 10
Aluminum crochet hook, Size G
Stitch holder
Yarn-embroidery needle

Gauge: 4 stitches and 5 rows = 1 inch

Note: In the following directions, only the right-side rows are indicated. All wrong-side rows are worked as they appear; that is, k the k sts and p the p sts.

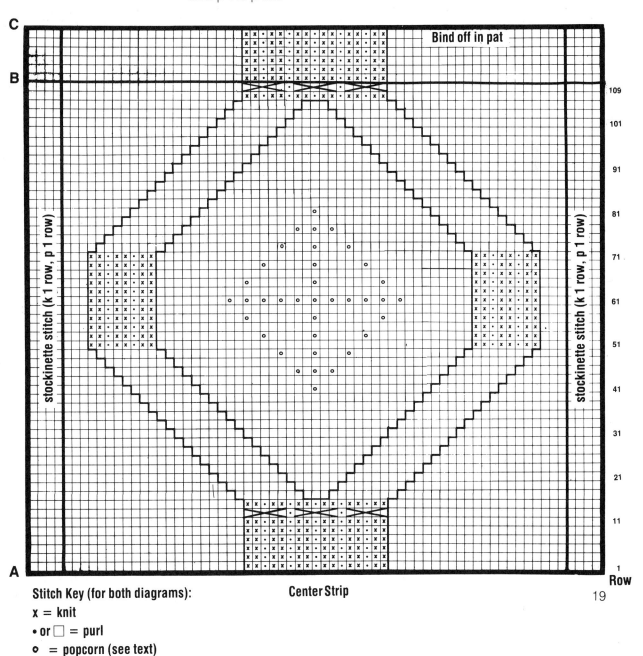

Center Strip

Stitch Key (for both diagrams):

x = knit

• or ☐ = purl

o = popcorn (see text)

✕ = cable (see text)

Note: For Rows 17-51 and 73-109, refer to text.

Center Strip: Cast on 67 sts. Then, following the chart, work the rows between A and B three times (1 through 109) and end with the rows between B and C, taking special note of the following rows:

Row 13: Work the center 17 sts of the row as follows: *Sl the first 3 sts on a holder. Holding them at the back of the work, k the next 2 sts, sl the last of the 3 slipped sts back onto the left-hand needle and p the st, k the 2 sts on the holder (cable made), p 1, rep from * once, and then work another cable in the same way on the last 5 sts.

Row 17: Following the chart, work the center 19 sts of the row as follows: To create the 8-st, diamond-shaped, raised border on the right-hand side, *sl the next p st on the holder and place behind the work, k the next 2 k sts, p the st on the holder, rep from * twice, and p the next st. To shape the left-hand border: *Sl the next 2 k sts on a

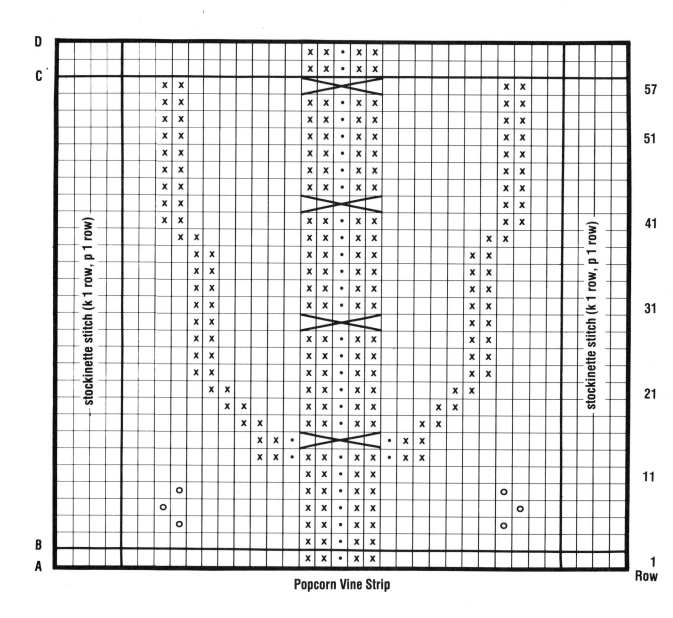

Popcorn Vine Strip

holder and place in front of the work, p the next st, k the 2 sts on the holder, and rep from * twice.

Rows 19 through 51: Following the chart, continue to work the 8-st raised border as for Row 17, working the pat on the center 21 sts on Row 19, the center 23 sts on Row 21, and continuing in this way, adding 2 more center sts on the right-side rows, as shown on chart, and at the same time adding 1 more p st on each side of the center p sts as the pattern progresses, working popcorn sts, as described below, where indicated on the chart.

To make a popcorn stitch: Sl the st to be worked onto the right-hand needle, turn the work to the wrong side, and k into the back lp of the sl st. Then p into the front lp of the same st, k into the back lp, and p into the front lp. Now turn the work to the right side and k each of these 4 sts, turn again, p each of the sts, turn once more, and sl the second, third, and fourth sts over the first. Finally, place the popcorn st on the right-hand needle.

Rows 53 through 71: Work even, following the chart.

Rows 73 through 109: Work as for Rows 17 to 51 but reverse the shaping on the right-hand and left-hand borders, thereby decreasing by 2 sts on each right-side row the number of center p sts, as shown on the chart.

Double-Seed-Stitch Strips: Make two: Cast on 34 sts. Then work as follows:

Row 1: K 4, *k 2, p 2, and rep from * across the row to the last 4 sts, k 4.

Rows 2 and 4: Work the sts as they appear; that is, k the k sts and p the p sts.

Row 3: K 4, *p 2, k 2, and rep from * across the row to the last 4 sts, k 4. Rep Rows 1 through 4 until the piece measures 60 inches. Bind off.

Popcorn Vine Strips: Make two: Cast on 35 sts. Following the chart, work as follows: Work the rows between A and C once; between B and C five times; and between C and D once. Work the cables and popcorns as on the center strip.

Finishing: Block each strip and then arrange them with a double-seed strip on either side of the center strip and a popcorn vine strip along each outside edge. Seam them together on the wrong side of the work with a running back st. Now work 1 row of sc around the entire piece, working 3 sc in each corner st as you turn.

Fringing: Cut a number of strands of yarn to measure 12 inches. Then, working around the edge of the afghan, *(knot 4 strands in the first sc, skip the next sc) three times, skip 2 more sc, and rep from * around. Then, around the afghan, tie a row of knots 1 inch from the edge of the afghan, using the set of fringe before and the set after the 3 skipped sc, leaving the remaining sets untied.

3
Diagonal
Rainbow

Approximate finished size:
46 by 58 inches

This brilliantly colored afghan is made of three strips, each
knitted on the bias in a stockinette stitch in eleven crayon
colors. The strips are then seamed together and edged
with a very narrow, royal blue stripe followed by a wider
band of medium blue.

Materials:

Knitting worsted:

    12 ounces in medium blue (A)
    4 ounces in royal blue (B)
    4 ounces in navy blue (C)
    4 ounces in red (D)
    4 ounces in light orange (E)
    4 ounces in peach (F)
    4 ounces in gold (G)
    4 ounces in yellow (H)
    4 ounces in light green (I)
    4 ounces in medium green (J)
    4 ounces in dark green (K)

Straight knitting needles, No. 8
Aluminum crochet hook, Size G
Yarn-embroidery needle

Gauge: 4 stitches = 1 inch

Color Sequence: *Strip 1:* *Work 12 rows of each color in a sequence of A through K; repeat from * to the desired length. *Strip 2:* *Work 12 rows of each color in a sequence of G, H, I, J, K, A, B, C, D, E, and F; repeat from * to the desired length. *Strip 3:* *Work 12 rows of each color in a sequence of B, C, D, E, F, G, H, I, J, K, and A; repeat from * to the desired length.

Strips: Make three: (Note: On the following strips, leave a 10-inch length of yarn at the beg and end of each color change for sewing.) Following the color pats for each strip as described above, cast on 3 sts and work in stockinette st (k 1 row—right side, p 1 row), increasing 1 st at the beg and end of every k row until there are 75 sts. P 1 row even (the sixth color in the sequence should have been completed). Continuing to inc 1 st on the left-hand edge of the work on every k row, dec 1 st on the right-hand edge on every k row. Continue in this manner, working in the proper color sequence, until the piece measures 55 inches. Then dec 1 st at the beg and end of each k row until 3 sts remain. Work 1 row even. On the last row, sl 2, k 1, pass 2 sl sts over; fasten off.

Finishing: Block each strip firmly to a rectangular shape and allow to dry in place. Then, with Strip 1 at the left edge, seam the three strips together with a running back st worked on the wrong side, matching the stripes and changing the color of the sewing yarn for each stripe. Now work 1 row of color-over-color sc around the piece, working 3 sc in each corner. With color B, crochet another row of sc around, working through only the back lps. Finally, with color A, work 7 rows of sc around the entire piece and fasten off.

4
Stitch
Sampler

Approximate finished size:
52 by 64 inches excluding fringe

Soft, heathery hues of mauve, sea foam green, blue marble, and gray flannel are worked in four different knitted stitches to make this afghan. The blanket is worked in eleven strips, each edged and then fringed in a warm charcoal brown.

Materials:
Heather tones of knitting worsted:
   16 ounces in mauve (A)
   12 ounces in blue marble (B)
    8 ounces in gray flannel (C)
    8 ounces in sea foam (D)
   20 ounces in charcoal brown (E)
Straight knitting needles, No. 10
Round knitting needle, No. 10
Yarn-embroidery needle

Pattern Stitches:
Pattern Stitch No. 1:
Rows 1 and 4: K.
Rows 2 and 3: P.
Repeat Rows 1 through 4 for pattern.

Pattern Stitch No. 2:
Rows 1 and 2: *K 2, p 2, and rep from * across the row.
Rows 3 and 4: *P 2, k 2, and rep from * across the row.
Repeat Rows 1 through 4 for pattern.

Pattern Stitch No. 3:
Row 1: *Sl 1 st as if to p, k 1, yo, psso the yo and the k 1, and rep from * across the row.
Rows 2 and 4: P.
Row 3: K 1, *sl 1 st as if to p, k 1, yo, psso the k 1 and the yo, and rep from * across the row, ending with k 1.
Repeat Rows 1 through 4 for pattern.

Pattern Stitch No. 4:
Row 1: *K the second st on the left-hand needle, k the first st, drop both sts from the left-hand needle, and rep from * across the row.
Rows 2 and 3: K.
Row 4: P.
Repeat Rows 1 through 4 for pattern.

Gauge in Pattern Stitches: On No. 10 needles for pat st No. 1: 7 stitches = 2 inches; on No. 10 needles for pat st No. 2: 3 stitches = 1 inch; on No. 10 needles for pat sts 3 and 4: 4 stitches = 1 inch

Strips: Working all strips to a length of 62 inches with straight needles, make four strips in pat st No. 1 with color A and three strips in pat st No. 2 with color B, both on 12 sts. Then make two strips in pat st No. 3 with color C and two strips in pat st No. 4 with color D, both on 14 sts.

Finishing: With color E and the round needle, pick up and k all sts along each long edge of each strip, making sure that the work is lying flat. Then, working back and forth, k 1 row and bind off. Arrange the strips in the color sequence of A, B, D, C, A, B, A, C, D, B, A. Seam the pieces together on the wrong side with an overcast st worked in color E. Then k 1 row on all sts across both the top and bottom edge of the afghan, bind off, and neatly sew each of the corners.

Fringing: Knot three doubled 13-inch strands of color E in every other st around the entire afghan.

5
Tweed
Geometric

Approximate finished size:
46 by 60 inches

Worked in a simple stockinette stitch with a garter-stitch border, this afghan consists of four triangles fitted together into a rectangle. The interplay of two different stripe patterns, worked in a red tweed, black, and white, creates a geometric pattern that is sophisticated yet one that is simple enough for a beginner to try.

Materials:

Knitting worsted:
  16 ounces in white
  12 ounces in red tweed
  6 ounces in black
Straight knitting needles, No. 10
Aluminum crochet hook, Size H
Yarn-embroidery needle

Gauge: 13 stitches = 4 inches in stockinette stitch

Triangle No. 1: Make two: With tweed, cast on 200 sts. Work in garter st (k every row) for 15 rows, decreasing 1 st at the beg and end of every third row (190 sts). Change to stockinette st (k 1 row—right side, p 1 row) and, decreasing 1 st at the beg and end of every row until 2 sts remain, work in color pat of 23 rows tweed, 13 rows black, 32 rows white, 15 rows tweed, and 12 rows black. Bind off the remaining sts.

Triangle No. 2: Make two: With tweed, cast on 150 sts. Work in garter st for 15 rows, decreasing 1 st at the beg and end of every third row (140 sts). Working a color pat of 26 rows white, 16 rows black, 60 rows white, and 14 rows black, dec as follows: *(Dec 1 st at the beg and end of every other row) four times, work 1 row even, dec 1 st at the beg and end of the next 3 rows, rep from * eight times more. Work 1 row even. Then, dec 1 st at the beg and end of each remaining row until 2 sts remain. Bind off the remaining 2 sts.

Finishing: Join the triangles as shown on the chart, sewing on the wrong side of the work with a running back stitch and matching the stripes. Block carefully.

6
Lacy
Ripples

Approximate finished size:
48 by 63 inches

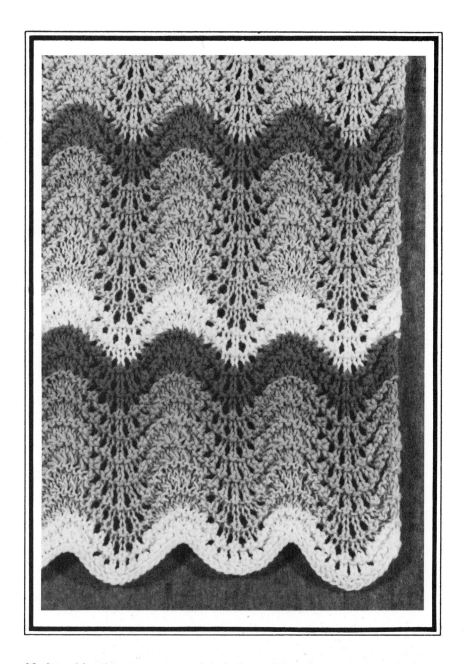

Knitted in the ever-popular fan-and-feather stitch, this ripple afghan is made in three strips worked in a design pattern of off-white, bisque, sand, coffee, and dark cocoa, which are then inconspicuously seamed together.

Materials:

Knitting worsted:
    6 ounces in off-white (A)
    6 ounces in bisque (B)
    14 ounces in sand (C)
    6 ounces in coffee (D)
    10 ounces in dark cocoa (E)
Straight knitting needles, No. 9
Yarn-embroidery needle

Pattern Stitch:

Rows 1 and 4: K.
Row 2: P.
Row 3: (K 2 tog three times), * (yo, k 1) six times, (k 2 tog) six times, and rep from * across the row, ending with (k 2 tog) three times.
Repeat these 4 rows for pattern.

Gauge in Pattern Stitch: 4 stitches = 1 inch

Strips: Make three: With A, cast on 84 sts. Then work in color pat as follows: *8 rows A, 8 rows B, 8 rows C, 8 rows D, 8 rows E*. Rep between *'s once. Then work (16 rows C and 8 rows E) three times and 16 more rows C. End by repeating the color sequence between *'s in reverse twice; bind off.

Finishing: Sew the strips together with an overcast st on the wrong side of the work, working color over color.

7
Geometric Quartet

Approximate finished size:
50 by 58 inches

Twenty knitted-on-the-diagonal squares, each composed of a solid and striped triangle, form an interesting geometric-patterned rectangle. The predominant color of this afghan is cocoa brown, accented with powder pink, aqua, and oyster.

Materials:

Knitting worsted:

    16 ounces in cocoa brown (A)

    16 ounces in aqua (B)

    8 ounces in powder pink (C)

    4 ounces in oyster (D)

Straight knitting needles, No. 10

Aluminum crochet hook, Size G

Yarn-embroidery needle

Gauge: 11 stitches = 3 inches; 18 rows = 3 inches

Squares: Make twenty: With color A, cast on 2 sts. Then work as follows:

Row 1: K, increasing 1 st in each st.

Row 2: P.

Row 3: K, increasing 1 st in the first and last sts. Continuing in stockinette st (k 1 row—right side; p 1 row), inc 1 st at the beg and end of every k row until there are 48 sts in all. P the next row. Change to color C and k 1 row, decreasing 1 st at the beg and the end of the row. Then work in reverse stockinette st (k on the wrong side; p on the right-side row), decreasing 1 st at the beg and end of every right-side row until 32 sts remain. Then work 1 k row on the wrong side of the piece. Change to color B and, working in stockinette st, continue to dec as established until 16 sts remain. P the next row. Change to color D and k the next row, decreasing 1 st at the beg and end of the row. Now work in reverse stockinette st, decreasing as before on the right side of the work, until 2 sts remain. Bind off. (Note: The unblocked squares will appear diamond-shaped, but with careful, firm blocking, they will shape into perfect 10-inch squares.)

Finishing: Block each square. Then edge each with a row of color-over-color sc, working 3 sc in each corner st as you turn and the same number of sc on each side. Join the squares on the wrong side, overcasting them through the back lps of the sc edging, arranging them four squares across and five down with the color-A triangles placed at the lower left-hand corner of each square. Then, with color A, satin-stitch a ½-inch diamond over each four-corner intersection between squares, as shown in the photograph. For the outer edging, work 1 row of color-A sc around the four sides of the joined piece, working 3 sc in each corner st and the same number of sts on corresponding sides. Then knit two border pieces for the long side edges as follows: With color B, cast on 16 sts. Work in reverse stockinette st for 57 inches, and bind off. Make borders for the top and bottom edges in the same manner, working these on 146 sts for 4 inches. With a running backstitch, sew the borders to the joined piece on the wrong side of the work, placing them so that the side borders extend 3½ inches out from each side edge of the joined piece and 3½ inches beyond it on the top and bottom edges. Now sew the top and bottom strips in place, leaving the extended edges of the side borders unjoined. With color A, work 1 row of sc along the inside edge of each of the four extended portions of both side borders. Sew these edged portions to the adjacent short edges of the top and bottom borders, overlapping the color-A sc edging onto the piece to which it will be joined. Finally, with color B, work 1 row of sc around the completed piece and then repeat with 2 rows of color A. Block the piece firmly.

8
Fair
Isle

Approximate finished size:
  48 by 59 inches excluding fringe

Three five-inch-wide Fair Isle vertical strips and four eight-inch-wide heather green ones are joined to form this afghan, which is fringed in a natural color. The other colors used are periwinkle and taupe.

Color Key:
o = MC
□ = A
x = B
• = C

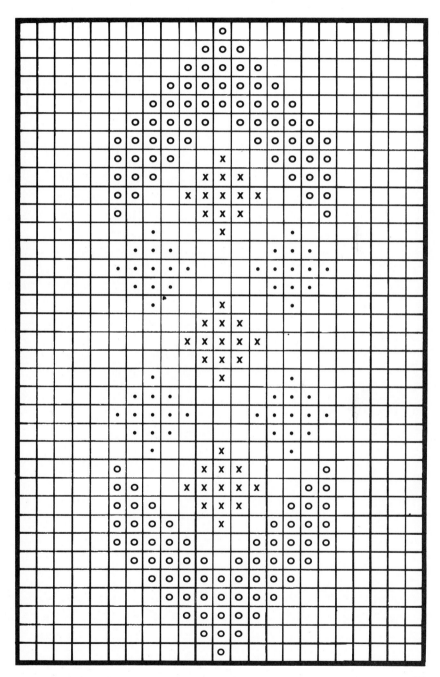

Materials:
Knitting worsted:
  28 ounces in heather green (MC)
  16 ounces in natural (A)
    4 ounces in periwinkle blue (B)
    4 ounces in taupe (C)
Straight knitting needles, No. 7
Aluminum crochet hook, Size F
Yarn-embroidery needle

Gauge: 4 stitches and 6 rows = 1 inch

Solid-Color Strips: Make four: With MC, cast on 34 sts and work in reverse stockinette st (p 1 row—right side, k 1 row) for 59 inches. Bind off.

Fair Isle Strips: Make three: With A, cast on 23 sts. Working in stockinette st throughout (k 1 row—right side, p 1 row), work even for 3 inches. Then work *35 rows of pat, following the graph, 6 inches of color A only, and rep from * three times more, ending with 35 rows of pat and 3 inches of color A. Bind off.

Finishing: Using an overcast stitch on the wrong side of the work, join the strips, starting and ending with a MC strip and alternating one MC solid-color strip with one Fair Isle strip between.

Edging: Work 1 rnd of color-over-color sc around the entire piece.

Fringing: Knot three 10-inch strands of color A in every other sc around the afghan.

9
Wedgwood

Approximate finished size:
  50 by 60 inches including edging

Designed in the colors and mood of Wedgwood chinas, this lovely afghan is knitted in seven easy-to-work pieces: three main strips, in ivory, which are sewn together to create the background of the piece; three edging pieces, in blue, which are joined to make the outer trim; and, finally, a large motif, also worked in blue, which is sewn to the center of the finished afghan.

Materials:
Knitting worsted:
    56 ounces in ivory (MC)
    16 ounces in Wedgwood blue (CC)
Straight knitting needles, No. 11
4 double-pointed needles, No. 9
Aluminum crochet hook, Size G
Yarn-embroidery needle

Pattern Stitch for MC Strips:
Row 1 (right side): Sl 1, p to end of row.
Row 2: Sl 1, k to end of row.
Repeat these 2 rows for pattern.

Pattern Stitch for CC Edging:
Row 1: K.
Rows 2, 4, and 6: P.
Row 3: K, increasing 1 st in each st across.
Row 5: K 1, *yo, k 2 tog, and rep from * across row, ending with k 1.
Repeat Rows 5 and 6 for pattern.

Gauge in Pattern Stitches: On No. 11 needles for strips and edging:
7 stitches = 2 inches

Gauge for Motif: On No. 9 needles: 4 stitches = 1 inch

Narrow Strips: Make two: With MC and No. 11 needles, cast on 34 sts. Work in strip pat until piece measures 54 inches and bind off.

Wide Strip: With MC and No. 11 needles, cast on 84 sts. Work in strip pat until piece measures 54 inches and bind off.

Edging: Make three: With CC and No. 11 needles, cast on 168 sts. Work in edging pat until piece measures 3½ inches. Bind off loosely.

Center Motif: With CC and four No. 9 dp needles, cast on 8 sts, placing 2 sts on the first needle and 3 sts each on the second and third needles. Join the needles into a round and k all sts through the back lps to keep the center flat.
Rnd 1: *Yo, k 1, and rep from * around (16 sts).
Rnd 2 and every other even-numbered rnd: K.
Rnd 3: *Yo, k 2, and rep from * around (24 sts).
Rnd 5: *Yo, k 3, and rep from * around (32 sts).
Rnds 7, 9, and 11: Rep as for rnds 1, 3, and 5, adding 1 more k st after each yo on each successive rnd (56 sts).
Rnd 13: *Yo, k 1, k 2 tog, yo twice, k 2 tog, k 2, and rep from * around.

On the next and all subsequent rnds, wherever 2 yo have been worked on the previous rnd, k 1 and then p 1 into the new sts.

Rnd 15: *Yo, k 8, and rep from * around.

Rnd 17: *Yo, k 9, and rep from * around.

Rnd 19: *Yo, k 1, k 2 tog, yo twice, (k 2 tog) twice, yo twice, k 2 tog, k 1, and rep from * around.

Rnd 21: *Yo, k 11, and rep from * around.

Rnd 23: *Yo, k 12, and rep from * around.

Rnd 25: *Yo, k 5, k 2 tog, yo twice, k 2 tog, k 4, and rep from * around.

Rnd 27: *Yo, k 4, k 2 tog, yo twice, (k 2 tog) twice, yo twice, k 2 tog, k 2, and rep from * around.

Rnd 29: *Yo, k 7, k 2 tog, yo twice, k 2 tog, k 4, and rep from * around.

Rnd 31: *Yo, k 1, yo, k 2 tog, k 3, k 2 tog, yo twice, (k 2 tog) twice, yo twice, k 2 tog, k 2, and rep from * around.

Rnd 33: *Yo, k 1, k 2 tog, yo, k 2 tog, k 4, k 2 tog, yo twice, k 2 tog, k 4, and rep from * around.

Rnd 35: *Yo, k 1, yo, k 2, yo, k 1, yo, k 2 tog, k 11, and rep from * around.

Rnd 37: *Yo, k 2, (yo, k 1, k 2 tog) twice, yo, k 2 tog, k 10, and rep from * around.

Rnd 39: *Yo, (k 1, yo, k 2 tog) three times, yo, k 1, yo, (k 2 tog) twice, yo twice, (k 2 tog) twice, yo twice, k 2 tog, k 1, and rep from * around.

Rnd 41: *Yo, k 2 tog, k 1, yo, k 1, k 2 tog, yo, k 2 tog, k 1, yo, (k 2 tog) twice, yo, k 2 tog, k 8, and rep from * around.

Rnd 43: *Yo, k 1, k 2 tog, yo, (k 2 tog) twice, (yo, k 1, k 2 tog) twice, yo, k 2 tog, k 7, and rep from * around.

Rnd 45: *Yo, (k 1, yo, k 2 tog) four times, yo, k 1, yo, (k 2 tog) twice, yo twice, k 2 tog, k 2, and rep from * around.

Rnd 47: *(Yo, k 2 tog, k 1) three times, yo, k 1, k 2 tog, yo, k 2, (yo, k 2 tog) twice, k 5, and rep from * around.

Rnd 49: *Yo, (k 2 tog) twice, yo, k 2 tog, (k 1, yo, k 2 tog) three times, k 1, yo, k 2, yo, k 2 tog, k 4, and rep from * around.

Rnd 51: *Yo, (k 2 tog) twice, (yo, k 2 tog, k 1) five times, yo, k 2 tog, k 3, and rep from * around.

Rnd 53: *Yo, (k 2 tog) twice, (yo, k 2 tog, k 1) five times, yo, k 2 tog, k 2, and rep from * around.

Rnd 55: *Yo, k 3 tog, k 1, (yo, k 2 tog, k 1) six times, and rep from * around.

Rnd 57: *Yo, (k 2 tog) twice, (yo, k 2 tog, k 1) five times, yo, k 2 tog, and rep from * around.

Rnd 58: K.

Bind off loosely.

Finishing: With the right side of the work facing, sew one narrow strip to each side of the wide center one with a running back stitch. With CC, crochet two chains long enough to cover the seams just made and sew them in place. Work 1 row of CC sc along the cast-on edge of the three edging strips, join the strips by seaming them along their short edges, and gather the joined strip along the sc row, using a length of CC long enough to fit around the afghan; sew it in place around the afghan. Finally, carefully block the center motif so that it lies flat and sew it in place in the middle of the wide center strip.

10
Tyrolean

Approximate finished size:
   48 by 60 inches excluding fringe

Reminiscent of the beautiful handwork produced in the mountainous Tyrolean region nestled in between Austria, Switzerland, Germany, and Italy, this afghan is made in alpine colors. Twenty eggshell-colored squares, knitted with a textured popcorn motif in the center of each, are reembroidered in cherry red and pine green, joined with those two colors, and then fringed in the cherry red.

Materials:

Knitting worsted:
    48 ounces in eggshell (MC)
    4 ounces in cherry red (A)
    4 ounces in pine green (B)
Straight knitting needles, No. 9
Aluminum crochet hook, Size H
Yarn-embroidery needle

Gauge: 4 stitches and 6 rows = 1 inch

Squares: Make twenty: With MC, cast on 43 sts. Then work as follows:
Row 1 (wrong side): K.
Rows 2 through 11: Work in reverse stockinette st (p 1 row—right side, k 1 row).
Row 12: P across 21 sts, (k 1, p 1, k 1, p 1) in the next st, transfer these 4 sts onto the right-hand needle, turn work, k 4, turn, p 4 tog (1 popcorn made), p across the remaining 21 sts.
Rows 13 through 17: Work in reverse stockinette st.
Row 18: P across 17 sts, (popcorn in the next st, p 3) twice, popcorn, p across the remaining 17 sts.
Rows 19 through 23: Work in reverse stockinette st.
Row 24: P across 13 sts, (popcorn, p 3) four times, popcorn, p across the remaining 13 sts.
Rows 25 through 29: Work in reverse stockinette st.
Row 30: P across 9 sts, (popcorn, p 3) six times, popcorn, p across the remaining 9 sts.
Rows 31 through 35: Work in reverse stockinette st.
Row 36: Rep Row 24.
Rows 37 through 41: Work in reverse stockinette st.
Row 42: Rep Row 18.
Rows 43 through 47: Work in reverse stockinette st.
Row 48: Rep Row 12.
Rows 49 through 59: Work in reverse stockinette st.
Row 60: Bind off.

Finishing of Squares: *Edging:* With MC, work 1 row of sc around each square, working 3 sc in each corner st as you turn. With B, work a second rnd in the same manner and a third with A. *Embroidery:* With A and B, embroider three- and five-petaled lazy-daisy-stitch (see Stitch Glossary) flowers on each square, following the chart for color and placement. Then, with B and a stem stitch (see Stitch Glossary), work a diamond-shaped "frame" around the popcorn design in the center of each square. Outline this embroidered frame with another one worked in color A.

Finishing of Afghan: With A and an overcast stitch, sew the squares into a rectangle that is four squares wide and five squares long. Fringe the outer edge by knotting fifteen strands of MC, each 16 inches long, in each corner of the completed afghan, at each point of the joining of the squares, and twice evenly spaced between each of the knotted groups already placed.

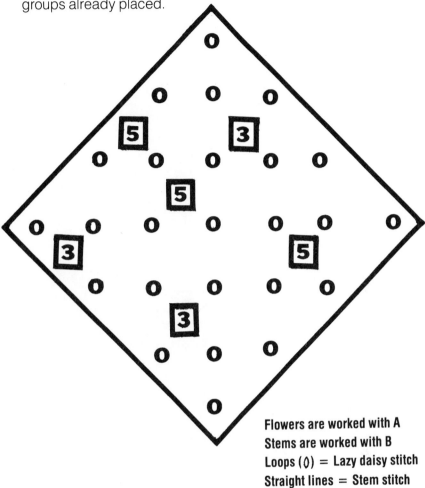

Flowers are worked with A
Stems are worked with B
Loops (◊) = Lazy daisy stitch
Straight lines = Stem stitch

Actual Size

11
Cathedral
Lace

Approximate finished size:
60 by 72 inches

This exquisite, oversized afghan is knitted in a cathedral-spired lace pattern. Worked in five jonquil-colored strips, the completed afghan is delicate, luxurious and light as a feather. Fringing and chains of embroidered white daisies concealing the four seams finish the piece.

Materials:

Sport yarn:
   48 ounces in jonquil yellow
    2 ounces in white
Straight knitting needles, No. 10½
Aluminum crochet hook, Size G
Yarn-embroidery needle

Cathedral-Spire Pattern Stitch:

Row 1: *K 1, yo, sl 1, k 1, psso, k 7, k 2 tog, yo, rep from * across, and end k 1.
Row 2 and all other even-numbered rows: P.
Row 3: *K 1, yo, k 1, sl 1, k 1, psso, k 5, k 2 tog, k 1, yo, rep from * across, and end k 1.
Row 5: *K 1, yo, k 2, sl 1, k 1, psso, k 3, k 2 tog, k 2, yo, rep from * across, and end k 1.
Row 7: *K 1, yo, k 3, sl 1, k 1, psso, k 1, k 2 tog, k 3, yo, rep from * across, and end k 1.
Row 9: *K 1, yo, k 4, sl 1, k 2 tog, psso, k 4, yo, rep from * across, and end k 1.
Row 11: *K 4, k 2 tog, yo, k 1, yo, sl 1, k 1, psso, k 3, rep from * across, and end k 1.
Row 13: *K 3, k 2 tog, (k 1, yo) twice, k 1, sl 1, k 1, psso, k 2, rep from * across, and end k 1.
Row 15: *K 2, k 2 tog, k 2, yo, k 1, yo, k 2, sl 1, k 1, psso, k 1, rep from * across, and end k 1.
Row 17: *K 1, k 2 tog, k 3, yo, k 1, yo, k 3, sl 1, k 1, psso, rep from * across, and end k 1.
Row 19: Sl 1, k 2 tog, psso, *k 4, yo, k 1, yo, k 4, rep from * across, and end k 1.
Row 20: K.
Repeat Rows 1 through 20 for pattern.

Seed-Stitch Pattern:

Row 1: *K 1, p 1, rep from * across, and end k 1.
Repeat for pattern.

Gauge in Pattern Stitch: 7 stitches = 2 inches in stockinette st (k 1 row—right side, p 1 row)

Strips: Note: On both the narrow and the wide strips, work all sts of the first 4 and the last 4 rows in seed st; also maintain the first and the last 5 sts in seed st throughout. Work the sts between as follows:
Narrow Strips: Make three: Cast on 35 sts. After the first 4 rows of seed st, work the cathedral-spire pat st on the center 25 sts. Continue until

the piece measures 71 inches, ending with a wrong-side row. After the last 4 rows of seed st have been completed, bind off.

Wide Strips: Make two: Cast on 47 sts. After the first 4 rows of seed st, work the cathedral-spire pat st on the center 37 sts. Continue until the piece measures 71 inches, ending with a wrong-side row. After the last 4 rows of seed st have been completed, bind off.

Finishing: Sew the strips together with an overcast st on the wrong side of the work, placing the narrow strips so that they become the outside edges and the center of the piece; the wide strips should be on each side of the center strip. Work 1 row of jonquil sc around the edge of the joined piece.

Daisy-Chain Embroidery (see Stitch Glossary): With white, evenly space eighteen lazy daisies along each of the four seams, placing them approximately 2½ inches apart. Then, with white, embroider a straight line of running chain sts between each two adjacent daisies to make stems. With jonquil, work a French knot in the center of each daisy.

Fringing: Cut a number of 5-inch strands of jonquil and forty-eight 5-inch strands of white. Knot two strands of jonquil in each sc around, attaching one set of 2-strand white fringe in each of the 3 sc at the top and bottom of each of the four lines of daisy embroidery.

12
Your
Coat
of Arms

Approximate finished size:
45 by 54 inches

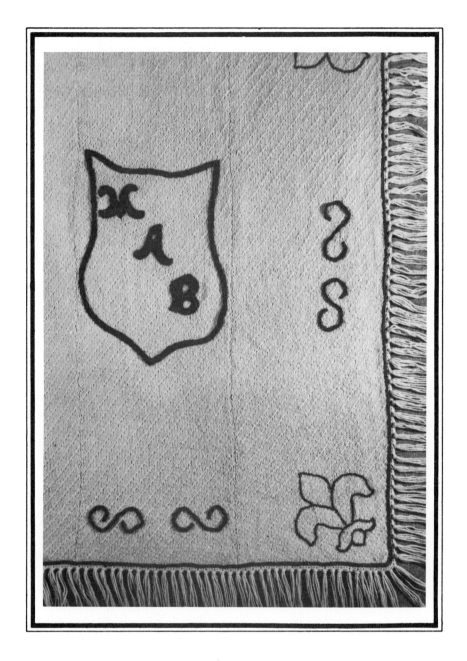

This knitted turquoise piece, made in three strips, features a large, embroidered three-letter monogram in the center, outlined with a shield in the same dark brown as the monogram. A border of scrolls and fleur-de-lis along the four edges completes piece.

Materials:
Knitting worsted:
   40 ounces in turquoise (MC)
    8 ounces in dark brown (CC)
Straight knitting needles, No. 9
Aluminum crochet hooks, Sizes H and I
Yarn-embroidery needle

Pattern Stitch:
Row 1: * K 3, sl 1, rep from * across.
Rows 2, 4, 6, and 8: P.
Row 3: *K 2, sl 1, k 1, rep from * across.
Row 5: *K 1, sl 1, k 2, rep from * across.
Row 7: *Sl 1, k 3, rep from * across.

Gauge: 4 stitches = 1 inch

Strips: Make three: Cast on 60 sts. Work even in pat st for 54 inches and bind off.

Finishing: Join the three strips together with a running back st on the wrong side of the work, matching the diagonal pat as well as possible. Then, with MC, work 1 rnd of sc around the entire piece, working 3 sc in each corner; join with a sl st to the first st. Still with MC, ch 2 and work 1 row of hdc around the entire piece, working 3 hdc in each corner; join with a sl st to the first st. Fasten off. With I hk and CC, crochet a chain long enough to fit around the afghan along the inside edge of the row of MC sc; sew it in place.

Scrolls, shields, and fleur-de-lis: Scrolls: Make eight: With CC and I hk, ch 56 and fasten off. Placing them 3½ inches in from the CC chain border, use the chains to form two scrolls for each edge, positioning them 2 inches apart over the center 12 inches of the side and arranging them in opposite directions (see photo). Enlarge or trace the shield, fleur-de-lis, and monogram patterns, following the pattern instructions, and cut them out. With CC and I hk, crochet a chain long enough to fit around the shield. Center the shield pattern on the afghan and sew the chain in place around the pattern; remove the pattern. Work a row of CC stem st (see Stitch Glossary) along both sides of the chain defining the shield. Space the monogram diagonally across the shield. With CC, work a row of stem st around each initial to define the outline and then fill them with a CC satin st (see Stitch Glossary). Place the fleur-de-lis pattern diagonally on one corner of the afghan, positioning it so that the apex points diagonally toward the center of the afghan and so that the bottom of the pattern is 3 inches in from the corner of the afghan. Work around it in CC stem st. Repeat to decorate the remaining three corners.

Fringing: Using 13-inch-long strands of MC, knot three strands in every third st around the edge of the afghan.

Each square = 1 inch

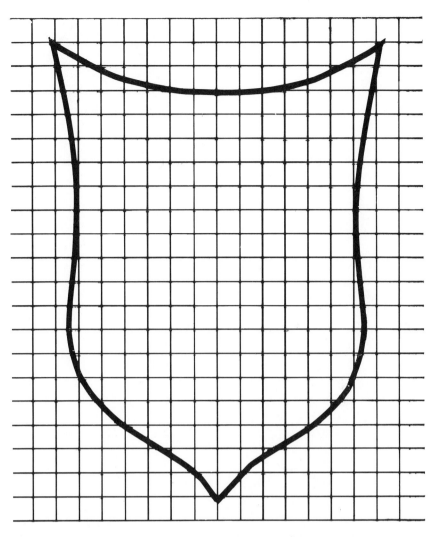

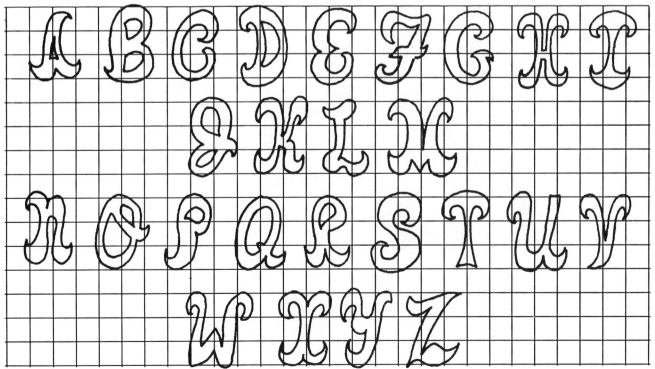

Reprinted from Fun with Felt *by Annette Feldman with the permission of the publisher, Van Nostrand Reinhold Company.*

Actual Size

50

Knitted Lap Robes

13
Warm
and
Furry

Approximate finished size:
41 by 50 inches

Knitted in a very simple open stitch, this shaggy, chocolate brown lap robe is strategically fringed with strands of yarn in the dark chocolate as well as with a closely color-related light coffee yarn to make an appealing, cozy, and very comfortable coverup for a late-fall excursion or a chilly night at home.

Materials:
Knitting worsted:
   36 ounces in dark chocolate (MC)
   12 ounces in light coffee (CC)
Straight knitting needles, No. 11
Aluminum crochet hook, Size J
Yarn-embroidery needle

Pattern Stitch:
Row 1: *Yo, sl 1 as if to p, k 1, and rep from * across the row.
Row 2: *Yo, sl 1 as if to p, k 2 tog, and rep from * across the row.
Repeat Row 2 for pattern.

Gauge in Pattern Stitch: 3 stitches = 1 inch

Background Strips: Make three: With MC, cast on 40 sts. Then work even in pat for 6 rows and even in stockinette st (k 1 row—right side, p 1 row) for 6 rows. Rep from * twelve times, ending with 6 rows of pat st. Bind off.

Finishing: Overcast the three strips together on the wrong side along the long edges.

Fringing: Starting at the bottom edge, knot two 15-inch strands of MC and two 15-inch strands of CC in every other long stitch of the first row of each 6-row pat-st section and in every other st of the first row of each stockinette-st section, mixing the colors at random and spacing them alternately on each row that is knotted. When you reach the top edge, turn the work around and knot that row in the opposite direction from the rest of the fringe. Trim the ends of the fringe evenly along the four edges of the afghan but leave the remaining fringe untrimmed for a shaggy effect.

14
Sunset

Approximate finished size:
  39 by 48 inches

Knitted in three vertical strips, which are later seamed together, this abstractly designed lap robe is worked in a
stockinette stitch combined with a richly textured stitch
and trimmed with color-over-color fringing. The colors
used—orange, sand, peach, and gold—are those of a
desert sunset.

Materials:
Knitting worsted:
    12 ounces in orange
    10 ounces in sand
    10 ounces in peach
    10 ounces in gold
Straight knitting needles, No. 10½
Aluminum crochet hook, Size I
Yarn-embroidery needle

Pattern Stitch:
Rows 1 and 3 (right side): P.
Row 2: *P 3 tog, (k 1, p 1, k 1) in next st, rep from * across.
Row 4: *(K 1, p 1, k 1) in next st, p 3 tog, rep from * across.

Gauge in Pattern Stitch: 4 stitches = 1 inch

Strips: (Note: When sts change from stockinette st on one row to pat st on the next row, as indicated on the chart, be sure to knit the first row of the pat st rather than purling it so that the color transition is smooth.) Make three different strips, following the accompanying charts. For Strip No. 1, cast on 8 sts with gold and then 44 sts with orange; for Strip Nos. 2 and 3, cast on 52 sts with orange. Work each of the strips to completion, working the orange and sand sts in the pat st and the peach and gold sts in stockinette st (k 1 row—right side, p 1 row). Bind off.

Finishing: Seam the strips together on the wrong side, using an overcast st and matching the designs. Work 1 row of color-over-color sc around the entire piece, working 3 sc in each corner.

Fringing: Using 13-inch-long strands in each of the four colors, knot three strands in every other st around, working color over color.

Strip No. 1

each square = 2 stitches and 2 rows
on the following three graphs

Note: Read all odd-numbered rows
on chart from right to left and
all even-numbered rows from
left to right.

56

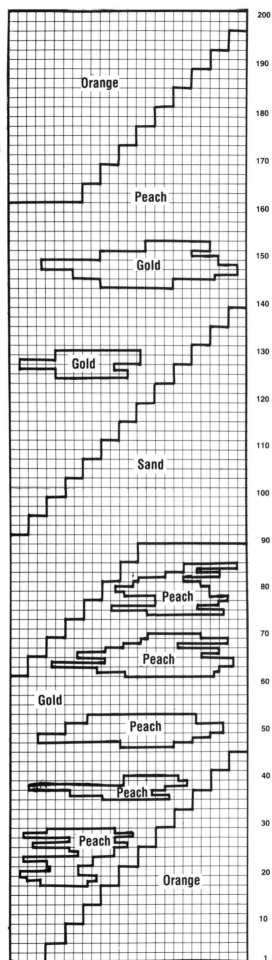

Orange

Peach

Gold

Gold

Sand

Peach

Peach

Gold

Peach

Peach

Peach

Orange

200

190

180

170

160

150

140

130

120

110

100

90

80

70

60

50

40

30

20

10

1

Row

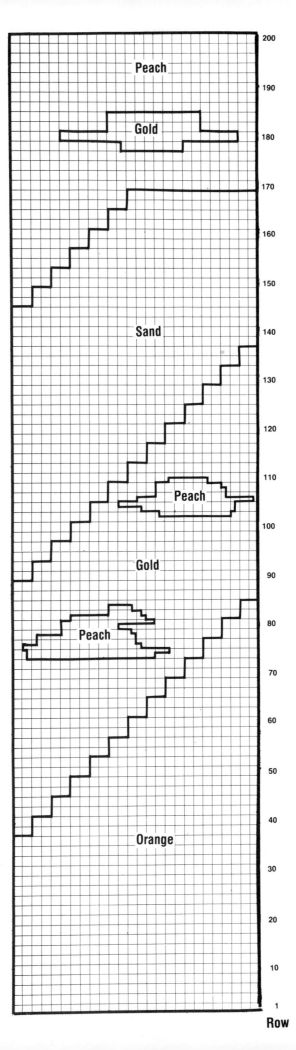

Strip No. 2

Peach

Gold

Sand

Peach

Gold

Peach

Orange

Row

57

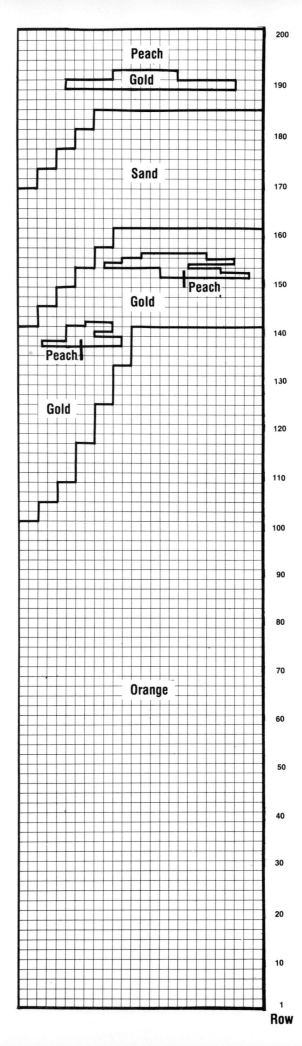

Strip No. 3

Peach

Gold

Sand

Gold

Peach

Peach

Gold

Orange

58

15
Winter
Warm-Up

Approximate finished size:
  40 by 53 inches

Take these six steaming cups of coffee along to keep you warm at a football game or in the ski lodge. Six of this afghan's bright red stockinette-stitch squares have a knit-ted-in "coffee cup" motif; the other six are made in reverse stockinette for contrast. Finally, curls of "steam" are cro-cheted with white and sewn on above the coffee cups.

Materials:
Knitting worsted:
　36 ounces in bright red
　4 ounces in white
　2 ounces in coffee
　2 ounces in black
Straight knitting needles, No. 8
4 bobbins (2 for bright red, 2 for black)
Aluminum crochet hook, Size G
Yarn-embroidery needle

Gauge: 9 stitches = 2 inches; 6 rows = 1 inch

Cup Squares: Make six: (Note: When working color changes according to the chart, work with separate bobbins of yarn so that the long strands of yarn need not be carried across the back of the work. When changing colors, be sure to twist yarns so that there will be no gaps between the sts.) With bright red, cast on 59 sts. Working in red throughout except for the cup motif, work as follows: Work even in reverse stockinette st (p 1 row—right side, k 1 row) for 6 rows. Continuing to work the first and last 5 sts of each row in reverse stockinette st and the center 49 sts in stockinette st (lk 1 row—right side, p 1 row) throughout, work 16 rows, complete the 29 rows of cup motif according to the chart, work 22 more rows, and finish by working 6 rows even in reverse stockinette st on all 59 sts. Bind off.

Reverse-Stockinette Squares: Make six: With bright red, cast on 59 sts. Work even in reverse stockinette st for 13 inches and bind off.

Finishing: With bright red, work 1 row of sc around each square, working 3 sc in each corner and an equal number of sc along each side. Join the squares according to the diagram, sewing on the wrong side with an overcast st and working through the back lps only of the sc sts. With bright red, work 1 row of sc around the joined piece.

C	R	C
R	C	R
C	R	C
R	C	R

Layout Diagram :
Cup-motif square = C
Reverse-stockinette square = R

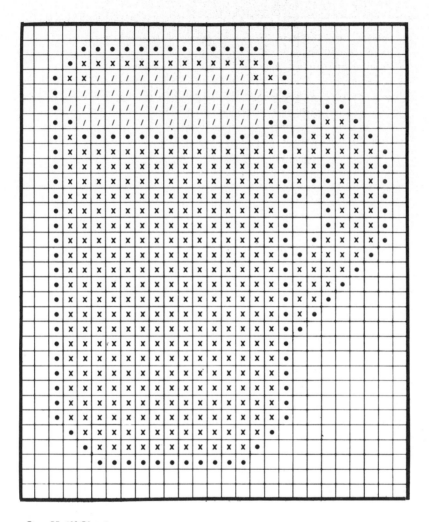

Cup-Motif Chart :

☐ = Bright red

/ = Coffee

• = Black

x = White

Note: Start first row of the cup motif on the 22nd stitch of the 49 stockinette stitches.

Seam Trim: With double strands of black, make four 53-inch chains and eighteen 13-inch chains; with double strands of white, make two 53-inch chains and nine 13-inch chains. Sew a 53-inch white chain over the two long inside seams; sew a long black chain on either side. In the same manner, sew the short chains over the horizontal seams.

Steam: With a single strand of white, make three short chains for each of the six cups. Arrange them to look like curls of steam (see photo), and sew them in place.

Fringing: Using 11-inch strands of bright red yarn, knot three strands in every third sc around.

Knitted Crib Blankets

16
Fleur-
de-Lis

Approximate finished size:
32 by 41 inches including edging

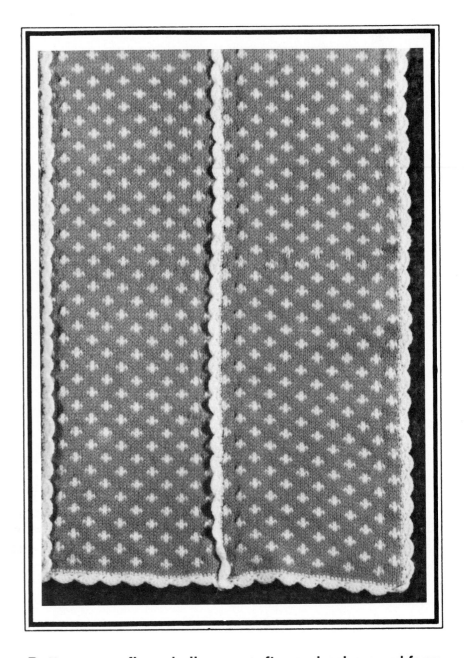

Butter-cream fleur-de-lis on a soft rose background form the "fabric" for this delicate-looking, knitted crib blanket, worked in five vertical strips and trimmed with a soft crocheted edging.

Materials:
Sport yarn:
  12 ounces in soft rose (MC)
  8 ounces in butter cream (CC)
Straight knitting needles, No. 2
Steel crochet hook, No. 1
Yarn-embroidery needle

Gauge: 7 stitches = 1 inch

Strips: Make five: With MC, cast on 45 sts. Working in stockinette st (k 1 row—right side; p 1 row) throughout, work 3 rows with MC. Then follow the chart, repeating Rows 1 through 8 until the piece measures approximately 40 inches. Complete the strip with 2 more rows of MC and bind off.

Edging: Crochet a CC edging around three of the strips as follows:
Rnd 1: Work in sc, working 3 sts in each corner as you turn and ending with a sl st in the first st.
Rnd 2: *Skip 2 sc, work 5 dc in the next sc, skip 2 sc, work 1 sc in the next sc, and rep from * around, ending with a sl st in the first st. Fasten off.

Work the edging in the same way at the top and bottom only of the remaining two strips, this time completing the first row of sc, then breaking off the yarn, and returning to the beginning of the row for the second row.

Finishing: Join the five strips on the wrong side with an overcast st, placing one of the three completely edged ones in the center and the other two at the outside edges and attaching them so that the edgings of the three completely finished ones overlap the plain edges of the other two.

Color Key:

□ = MC
o = CC

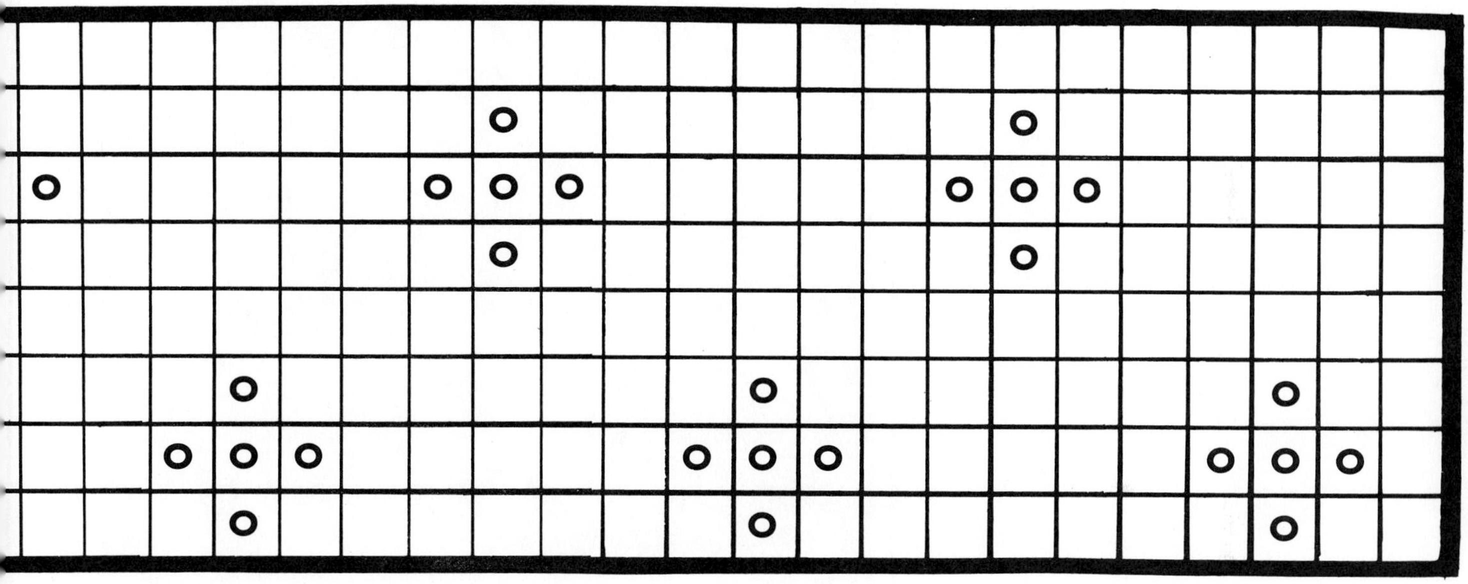

17
Mosaic Patchwork— A Reversible Crib Afghan

Approximate finished size:
36 by 38 inches

Bright-colored hexagons—aqua, coral, spring green, parfait yellow—are joined together to shape this interesting, geometric crib blanket. The individual pieces are worked in a simple knitted stitch and then edged in ivory. Once the main pieces have been fitted together, with small triangles completing the puzzle, the entire blanket is edged in ivory.

Materials:
Knitting worsted:
    8 ounces in aqua (A)
    8 ounces in ivory (B)
    4 ounces in coral (C)
    4 ounces in spring green (D)
    4 ounces in parfait yellow (E)
Straight knitting needles, No. 9
Aluminum crochet hook, Size G
Yarn-embroidery needle

Gauge in Stockinette Stitch: 4 stitches = 1 inch

Hexagons: Make nine in color A, six in color C, and four each in colors D and E: Cast on 16 sts. Working in stockinette st (k 1 row—right side, p 1 row) throughout, inc 1 st at the beg and end of every third row until there are 28 sts. Work 1 row even. Then dec 1 st at the beg and end of the next row and every third row thereafter until 16 sts remain. Bind off.

Color Key:
Aqua = A
Coral = C
Spring green = D
Parfait yellow = E

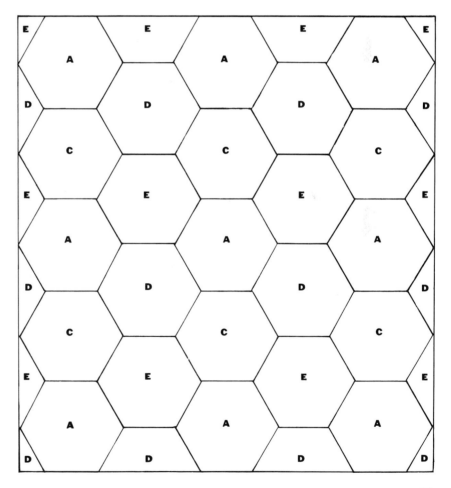

Triangles: Make four in color D and four in color E: Cast on 2 sts. Continuing to work in stockinette st, work 1 row even. On the next row, inc 1 st at the beg of the row. Work 2 rows even and then inc 1 st at the same edge on the next and every third row until there are 8 sts. Work 1 row even. Dec 1 st on the next and every third row on the same edge where the incs were made until 2 sts remain, work 1 row even, and bind off.

Corner Pieces: Make two in color D and two in color E, reversing the shaping on one of each set of two: Cast on 8 sts and work 1 row even. Then dec 1 st at the same edge on the next and every third row until 2 sts remain. Bind off.

Finishing: With the right side of the work facing, work 1 row of color-over-color sc around each hexagon, working 3 sc in each of the six corners as you turn. Then work 1 row of color-B sc around each of these pieces. Work around the eight triangular and four corner pieces in the same manner, but work along the inside edges only (the edges to be joined to the adjacent piece). Place all pieces in position, following the chart, and join them on either side of the work with color B and an overcast st.

Edging: With color B, work 4 rows of sc around the entire blanket, working 3 sc in each corner st as you turn and, on the first row only, 2 dc between the triangles and the corner pieces on both side edges so that the edging is even.

18
Parfait

Approximate finished size:
    28 by 40 inches including edging
    and fringe

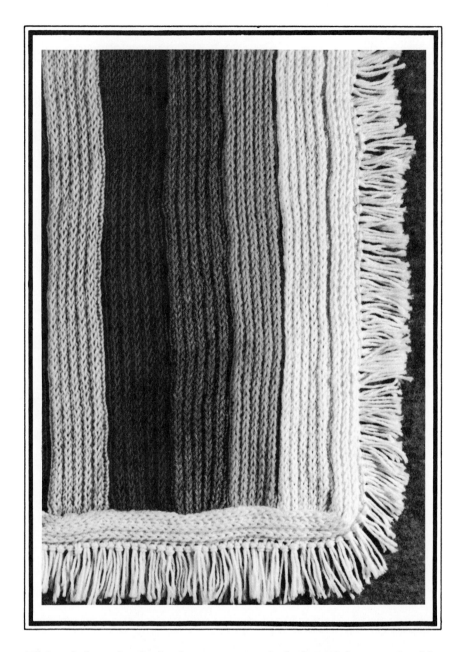

This afghan for baby is composed of nine strips worked in five happy "parfait" colors. They are knitted in a way that gives a raised, quilted effect to the piece, and when they are joined, they form a vertically striped design. The blanket is then finished with a solid-color, fringed edge.

Materials:
Knitting worsted:
    12 ounces in soft pink (A)
     8 ounces in lilac (B)
     8 ounces in bright pink (C)
     8 ounces in medium blue (D)
     8 ounces in light blue (E)
Straight knitting needles, No. 11
Yarn-embroidery needle

Pattern Stitch:
Row 1: P 2, *k 1, sl 1, and rep from * across the row, ending k 1, p 2.
Row 2: K 2, p to within the last 2 sts, k 2.
Repeat these 2 rows for pattern.

Gauge in Pattern Stitch: 5 stitches = 1 inch

Strips: Make one in color E and two in each of colors A, B, C, and D: Cast on 15 sts and work in pat st until the piece measures 36 inches; bind off.

Finishing: Sew the strips together lengthwise on the wrong side of the work, arranging them in order of A, C, B, D, E, D, B, C, A and using an overcast st.

Edging: Working with color A and in the same manner as for the other strips, work one strip 124 inches long (or enough to fit comfortably around all four edges of the joined piece). With the right side of the work facing, sew the edging strip around the afghan edges. Then fold the edging in half and sew the free edge to the wrong side.

Fringing: Cut 8-inch strands of color-A yarn and knot two in every st around the edge of the piece.

Crocheted Afghans

19
A
Garden
of Roses

Approximate finished size:
  51 by 60 inches

A large cluster of full-blown, appliquéd cerise and cardinal red roses and several delicate rosebuds, sitting among moss and avocado leaves with embroidered stems, is the dramatic focus of this richly textured, black afghan made in three sections invisibly sewn together. The theme is further carried out with a sprinkling of a few more rosebuds and leaves over the background. Finally, the piece is heavily French-fringed in black.

Materials:

Knitting worsted:

76 ounces in black (MC)

4 ounces in cerise (A)

1 ounce in cardinal red (B)

2 ounces in avocado (C)

4 ounces in moss (D)

Aluminum crochet hooks, Sizes G and K

Yarn-embroidery needle

Pattern Stitch:

Make a chain of the desired length.

Row 1: Ch 2, (1 sc, 2 dc) in the third ch from hk, *skip 2 ch, (1 sc, 2 dc) in the next ch, and rep from * across the row, ending with 1 sc in the last ch, ch 1, and turn.

Row 2: * (1 sc, 2 dc) in the next sc, skip 2 dc, and rep from * across the row, ending with 1 sc in the last sc, ch 1, and turn.

Repeat Row 2 for pattern.

Gauge in Pattern Stitch: On Size K hk: 3 stitches = 1 inch

Background Strips: Make three: With MC and Size K hk, ch 52. Then work even in pat until piece measures 60 inches. Fasten off.

Roses: Make two: With color A and Size G hk, ch 5 and join with a sl st to form a ring.

Rnd 1: Work *(1 sc, 1 hdc, 1 dc, 1 hdc, 1 sc) in the center of the ring, rep from * three times, and then join with a sl st to the first sc (four petals made).

Rnd 2: Ch 4, sl st in the starting ring under the center of the next petal, ch 4, sl st in the ring between this petal and the next petal, *ch 4, sl st in the ring under the next, rep from * once, ch 4, sl st in the ring between the next two petals, ch 4, sl st in the first ch of the starting ch-4 (6 lps).

Rnd 3: Work *(1 sc, 1 hdc, 2 dc, 1 hdc, 1 sc) in the first ch-lp and rep from * five times, ending with a sl st through the back lp of the first st of the previous rnd (six petals).

Rnd 4: Work *1 sc in the first sc of the previous rnd, 1 sc in the hdc, 1 sc in the next dc, 2 sc in the next dc, 1 sc in the hdc, 1 sc in the last sc of the petal, 1 sl st in the back lp of the next st on the previous rnd, and rep from * around five times.

Rnd 5: *Ch 5 and sl st between the next two petals of the previous rnd, rep from * five times more, ending with a sl st in the first st of the previous rnd.

Rnd 6: Work as for Rnd 3, working 3 dc in place of 2 dc on each petal.

Rnd 7: Work as for Rnd 4 except work the 2 sc in the center st of each petal, *working around the first petal with color A, the next petal with color B, and repeating from * around twice more.

Rnd 8: Ch 6, and work as for Rnd 5, working 6 ch instead of 5 ch throughout.

Rnd 9: Work as for Rnd 6, working 4 dc in place of 3 dc on each petal.

Rnd 10: Work as for Rnd 7, working in color A only and working 2 sc in each of the 2 center dc of each petal. Continue in this manner, increasing 1 more chain st on each ch-lp rnd and 1 more dc in the center of each petal rnd until 7 rnds of petals have been worked, alternating A and B on every other sc rnd only. Fasten off.

Rosebuds: Make thirteen: With color A and Size G hk, ch 3 and join with a sl st to form a lp.

Rnd 1: Work 8 dc in the center of the ring.

Rnd 2: Continuing around, work 1 dc in each dc around.

Rnd 3: *Ch 3, skip 1 dc, sl st in the next st, and rep from * three times more, ending with a sl st in the first skipped st at the beg of this rnd.

Rnd 4: *Ch 3, sl st in the next skipped st, rep from * three times, and end with a sl st in the last skipped st. Fasten off. To complete the shape of the rosebud, fold the bottom (the last row) of the bud up toward the head of the bud and lightly tack in place (see photo).

Leaves: Make fourteen: With color D and Size G hk, ch 5 and turn.

Rnd 1: Starting in the second ch from the hk, sc in each ch except the last, working 3 sc into it. Then sc along the opposite side of the chain, ch 1, and turn.

Rnd 2: Sc across 4 sc, work 2 sc in each of the next 2 sc, sc in each of the remaining 3 sts, join with a sl st in the first st, ch 1, and turn.

Rnd 3: Sc across 6 sts, sl st in the next sc, ch 3, sl st in the second ch from hk, sl st in the first sl st, sc to end of rnd, join with a sl st, and fasten off. Finish each leaf by embroidering the length of the center with color C and a stem stitch (see Stitch Glossary).

Finishing: Join the strips on the wrong side with MC and an overcast st. Then with Size K hk, sc around the entire edge of the joined piece, working enough sts along each side so that the piece lies flat and working 3 sc in each corner. Sew the two roses, three of the rosebuds, and four of the small leaves in one corner, as shown in the photograph. Sew the remaining rosebuds and leaves in place as desired. Then, with color C and a stem stitch, embroider stems on all the flowers as shown, using four strands for the large flowers and two for the buds.

Fringing: Cut strands of MC to 28 inches long. Knot four doubled-over strands in every third st around the piece. Then *knot four strands of the first group of fringe to four strands of the next group 1 inch below the original knot; rep from * around. In the same manner, work 1 more row of knots 1 inch below the last row. Trim the ends evenly.

20
Lady
Fingers

Approximate finished size:
   45 by 60 inches

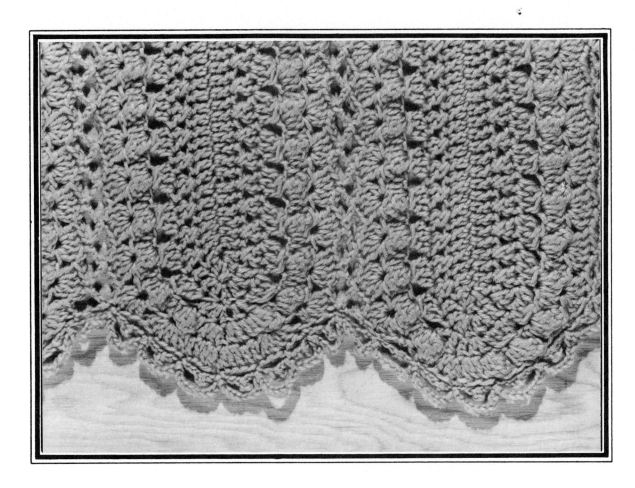

Seven long lady-finger-shaped strips, all in a soft shade of bisque, are made with five textured crochet stitches and then joined into this afghan. A border conforming to the top and bottom edges of the strips completes the blanket.

Materials:
Knitting worsted:
  48 ounces in bisque
Aluminum crochet hooks, Sizes G and I
Yarn-embroidery needle

Gauge: On Size I hk: 3 double crochet = 1 inch

Strips: Make seven: With Size I hk, ch 159. Then work as follows:
Rnd 1: Work 2 dc in the fourth ch from hk, * 1 dc in each ch across, and 5 dc in the last ch. Turn, and working along the opposite side of the starting ch, work 1 dc in each ch across, ending with 2 dc in the same ch as the first 2 dc of the rnd. Join with a sl st to the third ch of the turning ch-3.
Rnd 2: Ch 3, work 2 dc in the same st as the first ch at the base of the starting ch-3, 1 dc in the next dc, *skip the next st, 1 dc in the next st, 1 dc in the skipped st*, rep between *'s across to the second dc of the 5-dc group worked in the last ch of the starting ch on the previous rnd, work 1 dc in the next st, 5 dc in the next st, 1 dc in the next st, rep between *'s to the last dc of the previous rnd, work 1 dc in this st and 2 dc in the same st as the starting ch-3. Join with a sl st to the third ch of the starting ch-3.
Rnd 3: Ch 3, work 2 dc in the same st as the first ch at the base of the starting ch-3, ch 2, *work 1 dc in each of next 3 sts, keeping the last lp of each dc on hk, yo, draw through all 4 lps on hk, ch 2*. Rep between *'s to the third dc on the next 5-dc group, work 5 dc in this st, ch 2, and rep between *'s around. Then work 2 dc in the same st as the starting ch-3 and join with a sl st to the third ch of the starting ch-3.
Rnd 4: Ch 3, work 2 dc in the same st as at the beg of the previous rnds, 1 dc in the next dc, *(4 dc in next st, remove hk, insert in the first of 4 dc, pick up the dropped lp, pull through lp on hk [popcorn made]), 1 dc in each of the next 2 ch*, rep between *'s along one side of the piece up to the turning 5-dc of the previous rnd, work 1 popcorn in the first dc of the 5-dc group and 1 dc in the second dc, 5 dc in the third dc, 1 dc in the next dc, 1 popcorn in the next dc, and rep between *'s along the other side of the piece to within the last 2 dc, 1 popcorn in the next dc, 1 dc in the next dc, and 2 dc in the starting st of the rnd. Join with a sl st to the third ch of the starting ch-3.
Rnd 5: Ch 3, work 2 dc in the same st as on previous rnds, 1 dc in each of the next 3 dc, *5 dc in the st at the top of the next popcorn*, rep between *'s to the last popcorn on this side of the rnd, 1 dc in each of the next 3 dc, 5 dc in the next dc, 1 dc in each of the next 3 dc, rep from between *'s to within the last 3 dc, and end 1 dc in each of the next 3 dc. Join with a sl st to the third ch of the starting ch-3.

Finishing: With Size G hk, fasten the yarn in the third dc of the second

79

5-dc group to the left of the center point of the end of one strip. Then work as follows: Ch 3, join with a sl st to the third dc of the corresponding 5-dc group on the right side of another strip, ch 3, join with a sl st to the third dc of the next 5-dc group on the first strip, and continue in this manner, leaving the last 5-dc group on the side edge of each strip free. Fasten off. Join all strips in this same manner.

Edging: With Size G hk, join the yarn in the third dc of the 5-dc group to the left of the center 5-dc group on the last strip to the extreme left of the joined piece. Then work around as follows:
Rnd 1: *Ch 5, work 1 sl st in the third ch from hk (picot), ch 2, join with a sl st to the third dc of the next 5-dc group, rep from * along the outside edge of the piece to the last 5-dc group on the same side, **ch 5, picot, ch 2, skip 2 dc of the last 5-dc group, skip the next dc, sl st in the next dc, ch 5, picot, ch 2, sl st in the third dc of the next 5-dc group, and rep from ** once more. Then work (ch 5, picot, ch 2) once more, a sl st in the first st at the beg of the joining ch between strips, (ch 5, picot, ch 2) across the joining, sl st in the same st as the next sl st of the joining ch, and continue around, working across each strip end in the same manner and around the remaining long and short edges as established. Join with a sl st to the first st.
Rnd 2: * Ch 9, join with a sl st to the next sl st, and rep from * around.

From left to right: Lacy Ripples, p. 29; The Woven Plaid
Afghan, p. 95; An Irish Knit Afghan, p. 18.

From left to right: Warm and Furry, p. 52; Lady Fingers, p. 78;
Fair Isle, p. 34.

Top left from left to right: Winter Warm-Up, p. 59; Linked Chains, p. 126; Tyrolean, p. 41. *Top right from left to right:* Pinwheels, p. 121; Diagonal Rainbow, p. 22; Windswept, p. 92. *Bottom left from left to right:* Jigsaw, p. 105; Your Coat of Arms, p. 47; Geometric Quartet, p. 31. *Bottom right from left to right:* Bright Geometric, p. 134; Tweed Geometric, p. 27; The Earthtone Navaho, p. 129.

Minarets, p. 102

From left to right: The Bow-Knot Gingham, p. 138;
Wedgwood, p. 37; Woolly Friends, p. 141.

From left to right: Cathedral Lace, p. 44; Sunset, p. 54.

Top from left to right: A Garden of Roses, p. 74; Shadow and Substance, p. 16; Granny Goes Free-Form, p. 113.
Bottom left from left to right: Mosaic Patchwork, p. 68; Parfait, p. 71; Baby's Own, p. 144. *Bottom right from left to right:* Stitch Sampler, p. 24; Victoriana, p. 98; Pinstripes Overlaid with Lace, p. 89.

▶

From left to right: Ripples, p. 111;
Fleur-de-Lis, p. 64; Calico, p. 118.

21
Pinstripes
Overlaid
with Lace

Approximate finished size:
  48 by 60 inches excluding fringe

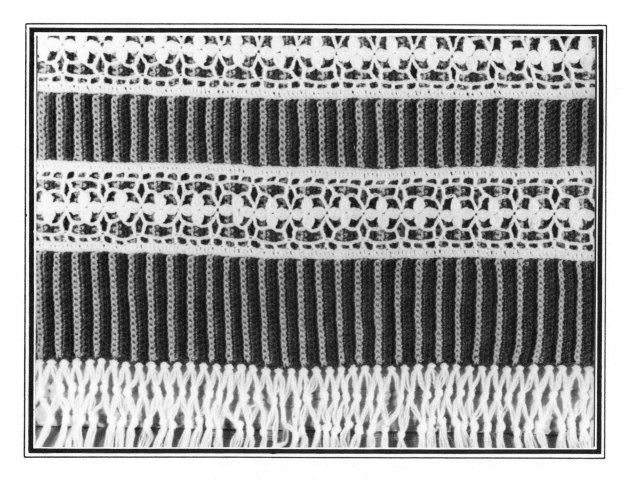

Here, strips of white crocheted lace are sewn onto a tex-
tured background of horizon- and captain-blue pinstripes.
Once the piece has been assembled, it is delicately
French-fringed in white around the entire outer edge.

Materials:

Knitting worsted:

32 ounces in horizon blue (A)

32 ounces in captain blue (B)

Sport yarn:

16 ounces in white (C)

Aluminum crochet hooks, Sizes G and I

Yarn-embroidery needle

Pattern Stitch for Pinstripes:

Make a chain of the desired length.

Row 1: Ch 1. Starting in the second ch from hk, work 1 sc in each ch across the row, ch 1, and turn.

Row 2: Working through the back lps of the sts, work 1 sc in each sc across the row, ch 1, and turn. Repeat Row 2 for pattern, alternating color A with B on every row.

Gauge: (Note: Be sure to stretch pieces to the proper width before measuring the length): On Size I hk for pinstripe pat: 7 stitches = 2 inches; Row 1 on Size G hk for lace-strip pat: 2 clusters = 2 inches

Pinstripe Strips:

Center Strip: With color B and Size I hk, ch 92. Then work in the pinstripe pattern for 48 inches and fasten off. (Strip should measure 26 inches wide.)

Side Strip No. 1: With color B and Size I hk, ch 60. Then work as follows: Sc the first 16 sts through both lps of the sts. Then work the next 10 sts in the pinstripe pat, the next 16 sts in sc through both lps of the sts, and the last 18 in the pinstripe pat. Maintain the pat throughout, working the piece to the same number of rows as the center strip. (Strip should measure 17 inches wide.)

Side Strip No. 2: Work as for the first side strip, reversing the order of the sts by starting with 18 sts worked in the pinstripe pat. (Strip should measure 17 inches wide.)

Lace Strips: Make four: Beginning at the narrow edge, ch 5 with color C and Size G hk.

Row 1: *(Yo twice, insert hk in the fifth ch from hk, yo and draw through, [yo and draw through 2 lps on hk] twice) three times, yo and draw through last 4 lps on hk (cluster made), ch 5, and rep from * forty-seven times. Ch 7 to end the last rep.

Row 2: *(Yo twice, insert hk in the same ch as the next cluster was made, yo and draw through, [yo and draw through 2 lps on hk] twice) four times, yo and draw through the last 5 lps on hk, ch 7, work 1 sc in the same ch as the next cluster was made, ch 7, and rep from * around the entire piece, ending with 1 sc in the top of the last cluster.

Row 3: Work 1 sl st in each of the next 3 ch, 1 sc in the same ch-7 sp, ch 11, * (1 trc in the next ch-7 sp) twice, ch 7, and rep from * across one long edge, ending with 1 trc in the last ch-7 sp, ch 5, and turn.

Row 4: * Skip 2 sts, work 1 dc in the next st, ch 2, and rep from * across the row, leaving the last 4 ch free, ch 3, and turn.

Row 5: * Work 2 dc in the next ch-2 sp, 1 dc in the next dc, and rep from * across the row. Fasten off. Repeat Rows 2 through 4 along the opposite long edge of the piece and fasten off.

Finishing: Sew the three pinstripe strips together with an overcast stitch on the wrong side of the work, matching the striped pat and placing the 18-st portions worked through the back lps of the sts to the outside edge of the piece so that they occur at the short ends of the afghan. Then work 1 row of color-B sc around the outer edge of the piece. Sew the four lace strips along the 16-st sc portions of the afghan worked through both lps of the sts.

Fringing: Cut a number of 20-inch strands of color C. Knot four doubled strands through every other stitch around the edge of the afghan. Then *knot four strands of the first group of fringe to four strands of the next, placing the knots 1½ inches below the original knots. Rep from * around, finishing with a second row of knots worked in the same way 1½ inches below the last row. Finally, trim the fringe to measure 3 inches below the last row of knots.

22
Windswept

Approximate finished size:
48 by 60 inches excluding fringe

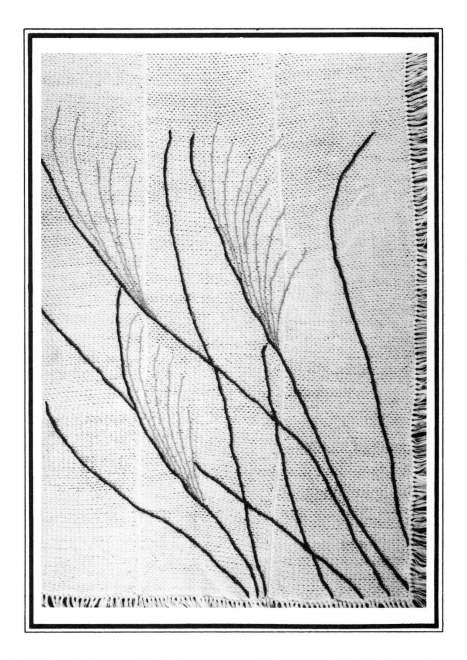

Delicate tangerine flowers on tall, graceful stalks sway across a crocheted, daffodil-yellow background—the afghan is worked in three textured strips and the flowers are embroidered on over the yarn.

Materials:

Knitting worsted:
- 56 ounces in daffodil yellow
- 2 ounces in avocado
- 2 ounces in moss green
- 2 ounces in tangerine

Aluminum crochet hook, Size J
Yarn-embroidery needle

Pattern Stitch:

Make a chain of the desired length.

Row 1: Starting in the fourth ch from hk, work 1 sc, *ch 1, skip 1 ch, 1 sc in next ch, and rep from * across the row, ending ch 2 and turn.

Row 2: Work *1 sc in the next ch-1 sp, ch 1, skip the next sc, and rep from * across the row, ending with 1 sc in the turning-ch sp, ch 2, and turn.

Repeat Row 2 for pattern.

Gauge in Pattern Stitch: 7 stitches = 2 inches

Strips: Make three: With daffodil yellow, loosely ch 60. Then work in pat for 60 inches and fasten off.

Finishing: Work 1 row of sc around each strip, working 3 sc in each corner st as you turn. Sew the strips together lengthwise on the wrong side of work, using an overcast st and sewing through the back lps only of the sc sts.

Embroidery: Work the embroidery in a stem stitch (see Stitch Glossary) as follows: Enlarge the pattern to actual size on tissue (see p. 12) and then transfer the design to the afghan with long basting stitches worked through the tissue. Tear away the paper and embroider over the basting stitches, following the pattern for color.

Fringing: Knot three 12-inch strands of yellow yarn in every other stitch around the entire outer edge of the afghan.

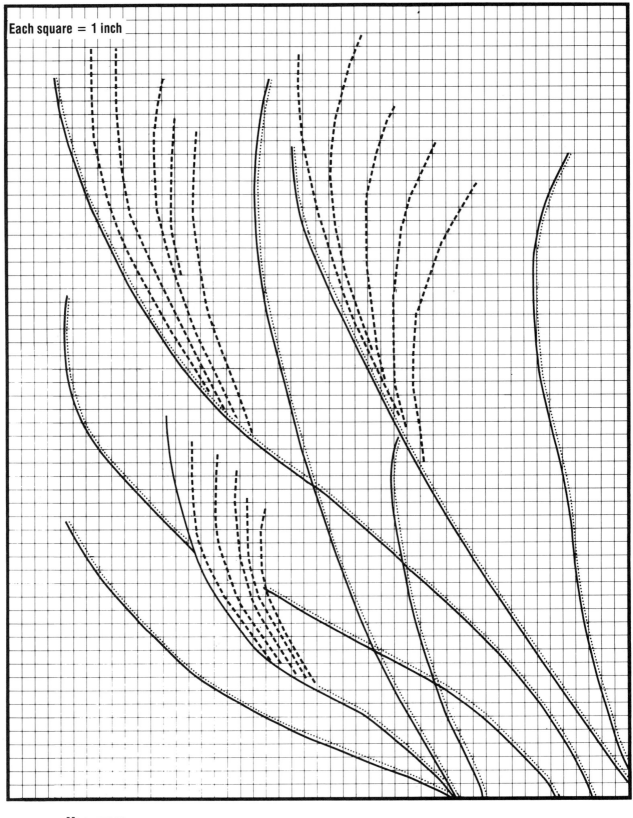

Each square = 1 inch

—— = Moss green

••••• = Avocado green

----- = Tangerine

23
The Woven Plaid Afghan

Approximate finished size:
51 by 60 inches excluding fringe

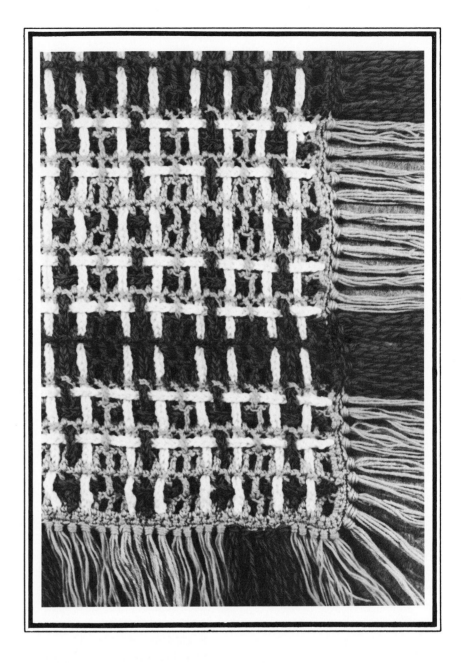

Worked in sand, burnt orange, sienna tweed, and off-white, this crocheted afghan is made in wide bands of triple-crochet filet mesh and then woven through with lengths of single-crochet chains to give a highly textured, plaid-patterned effect.

Materials:
Knitting worsted:
> 12 ounces in sand (A)
> 16 ounces in burnt orange (B)
> 20 ounces in sienna tweed (C)
> 20 ounces in off-white (D)

Aluminum crochet hook, Size I
Yarn-embroidery needle

Pattern Stitch:
Row 1: Starting in the seventh ch from hk, *work 1 trc, ch 1, and skip 1 ch. Rep from * across the row, ending with 1 trc in the last ch, ch 4, and turn.

Row 2: (Skip the first trc and ch 1), *work 1 trc in the next trc, ch 1. Rep from * across the row, ending with 1 trc in the third ch of the turning ch-4, ch 4, and turn.

Repeat Row 2 for pattern.

Gauge in Pattern Stitch: (trc and ch 1) five times = 3 inches

Foundation Strips: Make three: With color A, ch 57. Working in pat st throughout, work in color sequence of 3 rows A, *3 rows B, 3 rows C, 3 rows B, and 3 rows A. Rep from * five times more. Fasten off. On the wrong side of the work, join the three strips together vertically, matching colors and using an overcast st.

Vertical Weaving: Using chains made of double strands of yarn for all weaving, work as follows: Starting with color D, make a chain long enough to weave through the entire length (approximately 60 inches) of the piece. Starting at the lower right-hand corner, tack the end of the chain in place in the first ch-1 sp. Then weave over the first horizontal bar after the starting chain and under the next horizontal bar. Continue in this manner until the chain has been woven through the length of the piece; tack the chain in position. With color C, weave a chain along the next line of vertical spaces in the same manner, this time weaving under the horizontal bar over which the first chain was woven and over the next one under which the first was woven. Then work one more color-D chain as the first. To continue the vertical weaving, * skip the next two vertical lines of spaces, weave one color-D chain in the next vertical line, one color-C chain in the next, and one color-D chain in the next. Rep from * across the width of the piece.

Horizontal Weaving: Starting at the lower right-hand corner and working along the second row of each set of three color-A rows, *weave a color-C chain (making the chains the width of the piece and tacking each end as with the vertical ones) under the first vertical color-D chain, over the next color-C chain, under the next vertical color-D chain, and under the next color-A trc between the next two skipped spaces. Rep from * across the width of the piece, ending the row by weaving under the color-D chain, over the color-C chain, and under the color-D chain. Now, on the first and third rows of each set of three color-B rows, * work a color-D chain over the first vertical color-D chain, under the next vertical color-C chain, over the next color-D chain, and under the color-B trc between the next two skipped spaces. Rep from * across the row, ending the row by weaving over the color-D chain, under the color-C chain, and over the last color-D chain. On each center color-B row, weave a color-C chain as on the second of the color-A rows. (Note: There are no horizontal chains worked on the color-C foundation rows.)

Finishing: When all weaving has been completed, work 1 row of color-over-color sc around the edge of the entire piece, working through the ends of the woven chains as you go to secure them and working 3 sc in each corner.

Fringing: Working color over color, knot three 12-inch strands of yarn along the long edges, spacing and knotting five groups of fringe on the edges of the color-A stripes, four groups on the color B, and five on the color C. Then work along each of the short edges, starting in the lower right-hand corner with * five sets of color-B fringe, five groups of color C, five groups of color B, and five groups of color A. Rep from * across, ending with five groups of color B, five groups of color C, and five groups of color B, randomly spacing each group of five sets over 8 sc edging sts along each short edge.

24
Victoriana

Approximate finished size:
  60 by 60 inches including edging

Twenty-five crocheted squares—some very lacy, some simply textured—are joined together, checkerboard-fashion, to shape this handsome, traditional-looking afghan. It's made in a soft white wool, and its charm is further enhanced by a delicate edging.

Materials:

Sport yarn:
42 ounces in white
Aluminum crochet hook, Size F
Yarn-embroidery needle

Pattern Stitch:

Make a chain of the desired length.

Row 1: Ch 2, yo, insert hk in the third ch from hk, yo and draw through, yo, insert hk in next ch, yo and draw through, yo and draw through 5 lps on hk, *ch 1, yo, insert hk in the next ch, yo and draw through, yo and insert hk in the next ch, yo and draw through 5 lps on hk, and rep from * across the row, ending ch 3 and turn.

Row 2: Yo, insert hk in the third ch from hk, yo and draw through, yo, insert hk in the next ch-1 sp, yo and draw through, yo and draw through 5 lps on hk, * ch 1, yo, insert hk in the same ch-1 sp, yo and draw through, yo, insert hk in the next ch-1 sp, yo and draw through, yo and draw through 5 lps on hk. Rep from * across the row, ending ch 1, yo, insert hk in same ch-1 sp, yo and draw through, yo, insert hk in turning ch of previous row, yo and draw through, yo and draw through 5 lps on hk, ch 3, and turn.

Repeat Row 2 for pattern.

Gauge in Pattern Stitch: 5 stitches = 2 inches

Textured Squares: Make thirteen: Ch 54 and work in pat st for 11½ inches. Then work 1 row of sc around the outer edge of the piece, working 3 sc in each corner st as you turn and the same number of sc between corners. Fasten off.

Lacy Squares: Make twelve: Starting at the center, ch 8, join with a sl st to form a ring, and then work as follows:

Rnd 1: Ch 4, work 27 trc in the center of the ring, and join with a sl st to the top of the ch-4.

Rnd 2: Ch 5, skip the joining, *trc in the next trc, ch 1, and rep from * around. Join with a sl st to the fourth ch of the ch-5.

Rnd 3: In the first sp, work a sl st, ch 1, and sc. Then *ch 3, sc in the next sp, and rep from * around. End with a ch-1 and a hdc in the first sc to form the last lp (28 lps).

Rnd 4: Ch 3, dc in the same lp, *ch 5, skip the next 2 lps, 9 dc in the next lp, ch 5, skip the next 2 lps and, holding back on hk the last lp of each dc, work 2 dc in the next lp, yo, draw through all 3 lps on hk (cluster made), ch 3, cluster in the next lp. Rep from * around, ending with ch 3; join with a sl st to the first dc.

Rnd 5: Ch 3, dc in joining, *ch 5, (trc in next dc, ch 1) eight times, trc in the next dc, (ch 5, cluster in the tip of the next cluster) twice, and rep from * around, ending with ch 5; join as before.

Rnd 6: Ch 3, dc in joining, *ch 5, (sc in the next ch-1 sp, ch 3) seven times, sc in the next sp, ch 5, cluster in the tip of the next cluster, ch 7 for corner lp, cluster in the tip of the next cluster. Rep from * around, ending with ch 7; join.

Rnd 7: Ch 3, dc in joining, *ch 5, (sc in the next ch-3 lp, ch 3) six times, sc in the next lp, ch 5, cluster in the tip of the next cluster, ch 5, work (2 dc, ch 5, 2 dc) in the next corner lp, ch 5, cluster in the tip of the next cluster. Rep from * around, ending with (2 dc, ch 5, 2 dc) in the last lp, ch 5, and join.

Rnd 8: Ch 3, dc in joining, *ch 5, (sc in next ch-3 lp, ch 3) five times, sc in the next lp, ch 5, cluster in the tip of the next cluster, ch 5, dc in each of the next 2 dc, work (2 dc, ch 5, 2 dc) in the next ch-5 lp, dc in each of the next 2 dc, ch 5, cluster in the tip of the next cluster. Rep from * around, ending with ch 5. Join.

Rnd 9: Ch 3, dc in joining, *ch 5, (sc in the next ch-3 lp, ch 3) four times, sc in the next lp, ch 5, cluster in the tip of the next cluster, ch 5, dc in each of the next 4 dc, work (2 dc, ch 5, 2 dc) in the next ch-5 lp,

L = **Lace squares**
☐ = **Solid squares**

	L		L	
L		L		L
	L		L	
L		L		L
	L		L	

dc in each of the next 4 dc, ch 5, cluster in the tip of the next cluster. Rep from * around, ending with dc in each of the last 4 dc. Ch 5, and join.

Rnd 10: Ch 3, dc in joining, *ch 9, and holding back on hk the last lp of each trc, work 1 trc in each of the next four ch-3 lps, yo and draw through all 5 lps on hk, ch 9, cluster in the tip of the next cluster, ch 5, dc in each of the next 4 dc, ch 5, skip the next 2 dc, work (2 dc, ch 7, 2 dc) in the next ch-5 lp, ch 5, skip the next 2 dc, dc in each of the next 4 dc, ch 5, cluster in the tip of the next cluster. Rep from * around, ending with a dc in each of the last 4 dc. Ch 5 and join. Work 1 rnd of sc around each square, working 3 sc in each corner st as you turn and the same number of sts between corners. Fasten off.

Finishing: Join the squares as shown on the diagram, sewing on the wrong side of the work with an overcast st.

Edging: *Rnd 1:* Join the yarn in any corner st. Then work *ch 3, skip 1 sc, 1 sc in next sc, and rep from * around, skipping sc as necessary so that there are exactly twenty-eight ch-3 lps on the edge of each square. Join this rnd with a sl st to the first st.

Row 2: Now, working back and forth on consecutive groups of seven ch-3 lps, sl st in the first ch of the next ch-3 lp, sc in the same lp, *ch 3, sc in the next ch-3 lp, rep from * five times, and turn.

Rows 3 and 4: Work as for Row 2, working one less repeat on each consecutive row.

Row 5: Sl st in the first ch of the next ch-3 lp, ch 3, and holding the last lp of each trc on hk, work 1 trc in each of the next three ch-3 lps, yo, draw through all lps, and fasten off. Rep Rows 2 through 5 on each group of seven ch-3 lps around the entire afghan, joining the yarn for each new group in the second ch of the next unworked ch-3 lp.

25
Minarets

Approximate finished size:
47 by 60 inches

Three afghan-stitch strips in a biscuit tone are crocheted and joined together to become the canvas for an overall cross-stitch design suggestive of Middle-Eastern minarets. The pattern is worked in the unusual accent colors of taupe, forest green, and magenta.

Materials:

Sport yarn:

    28 ounces in biscuit (MC)

     6 ounces in magenta (A)

     6 ounces in taupe (B)

     6 ounces in forest green (C)

Afghan hook, Size L

Aluminum crochet hook, Size I

Yarn-embroidery needle

Pattern Stitch:

Make a chain of the desired length.

Row 1: First half: Ch 1, insert hk in the second ch from hk, yo and draw through, * insert hk in the next ch, yo and draw through, and rep from * across. Second half: Yo and draw through the first lp on hk, * yo and draw through 2 lps on hk, and rep from * across.

Row 2: First half: Ch 1, skip the first vertical bar, *insert hk from right to left under the top strand of the next vertical bar, yo and draw through, and rep from * across, ending by inserting the hk under both strands of the last vertical bar, yo and draw through. Second half: Yo and draw through the first lp on hk, *yo and draw through 2 lps on hk, and rep from * across.

Repeat Row 2 for pattern.

Gauge: 7 stitches = 2 inches; 14 rows = 5 inches

Strips: Make three: With afghan hk and MC, ch 54. Work even in pat st for 172 rows. Fasten off.

Finishing: With I hk and MC, join the strips as follows: Place two strips side by side. Make a sl st on the hk and then, starting from the bottom, *insert the hk from right to left through the corresponding first vertical bars on each side of the seam, yo and draw through the two vertical bars, yo and draw through the 2 lps on hk, and rep from *, working up the seam on each successive pair of sts along each side of the seam and being careful not to pull the sts too tight. When the seam has been completed, fasten off and repeat to join the remaining strip. Work 1 row of MC sc around the entire piece, working 3 sc in each corner, and join with a sl st to the first sc. Then work 1 row of reverse sc with MC (work as for sc but work from left to right) around the entire piece and join with a sl st to the first st. Fasten off.

Embroidery: Skip the first row of pat sts around the edge of the afghan. Then work 4 rows of color-A cross-stitch (see Stitch Glossary) around the entire blanket. Skip 2 more rows of afghan sts and work 4 rows of color-B cross-stitch around. Skip 2 more rows of afghan sts

Color Key:

• = A
/ = B
x = C

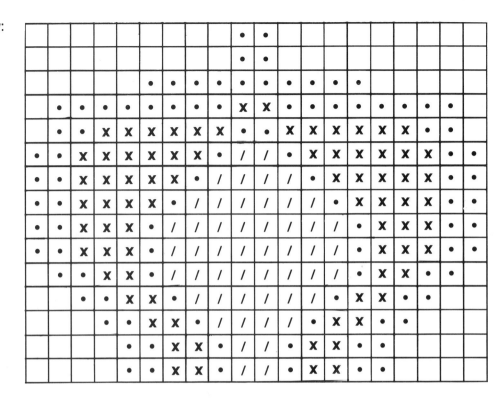

Minaret Design

and work 4 rows of color-C cross-stitch around. Skip 15 rows of afghan sts and work 2 rows of color-C cross-stitch. Skip 2 rows and work 2 rows color-B cross-stitch. Skip 2 rows and work 2 rows color-A cross-stitch. In the very center of the afghan, work a 4-st square of color-A cross-stitch. Surround it with 2 rows of color-B cross-stitch and then 2 rows color C. Now, following the chart, cross-stitch the minaret design in the 15-row space between the color-C stripes, evenly spacing five repeats of it along each long side and four repeats along each short side and working the design so that the points are toward the edge of the afghan. Finally, on each of the four edges of the center cross-stitch square, center and work one repeat of the minaret design, again with the points toward the edge of the afghan.

26
Jigsaw

Approximate finished size:
  44 by 66 inches

**Two giant-size granny squares and six rectangles, croche-
ted in stripes of turquoise, sea green, lavender, and off-
white, are joined jigsaw-puzzle-style to create an overall
pattern that is framed by a 3-inch-wide turquoise border.
The design and dimensions of the finished work make it
very adaptable for use as an area rug.**

Materials:
Knitting worsted:
  20 ounces in turquoise (MC)
   8 ounces in lavender (A)
   8 ounces in sea green (B)
   8 ounces in off-white (C)
Aluminum crochet hook, Size I

Gauge: 3 double crochet = 1 inch; 8 rows = 5 inches

Granny Squares: Make two: With color A, ch 6. Join with a sl st to form a ring.

Rnd 1: Ch 2, (yo, insert hk in the center of the ring, yo and draw through, yo and draw through 1 lp on hk, yo and draw through 2 lps on hk) twice, yo and draw through last 3 lps on hk, *ch 5, (yo, insert hk in the center of the ring, yo and draw through, yo and draw through 1 lp on hk, yo and draw through 2 lps on hk) three times, yo and draw through last 4 lps on hk (cluster made), ch 2, 1 cluster, rep from * twice, and end ch 5, 1 cluster, ch 2, and join with sl st to the second ch of the starting ch-2.

Rnd 2: Work 1 sl st in the next st, 1 sl st in the next ch-5 sp, ch 2, (yo, insert hk in the same ch-5 sp, yo and draw through, yo and draw through 1 lp on hk, yo and draw through 2 lps on hk) twice, yo and draw through last 3 lps on hk, *ch 2, 1 cluster in same ch-5 sp, ch 2, 3 dc in next ch-2 sp, ch 2, 1 cluster in next ch-5 sp, rep from * twice, and end ch 2, 1 cluster in same ch-5 sp, ch 2, 3 dc in next ch-2 sp, ch 2, join with sl st to second ch of starting ch-2.

Rnd 3: Work 1 sl st in next st, 1 sl st in the next ch-2 sp, ch 2, (yo, insert hk in the same ch-5 sp, yo and draw through, yo and draw through 1 lp on hk, yo and draw through 2 lps on hk) twice, yo and draw through last 3 lps on hk, *ch 2, 1 cluster in the same ch-2 sp, ch 2, 2 dc in the next ch-2 sp, 1 dc in each dc of the next dc-group, 2 dc in the next ch-2 sp, ch 2, 1 cluster in the next ch-2 sp, rep from * twice, and end ch 2, 1 cluster in the same ch-2 sp, ch 2, 2 dc in the next ch-2 sp, 1 dc in each dc of the next dc-group, 2 dc in the next ch-2 sp, ch 2, and join with a sl st to the second ch of the starting ch-2. Fasten off.

Rnd 4: With color C, join yarn in the first ch-2 sp and work as for Rnd 3, beginning with the starting ch-2. (Note: When changing to a new color, work the first row only of the new color in the back lps of the previous row; work the corners in the usual manner.)

Repeat Rnd 3 for pattern, working 3 more rows with color C, 4 rows with MC, and 4 rows with B. Fasten off.

Rectangle No. 1: Make two following the chart; then make two more, reversing the color pattern. With MC, ch 61. Change to color B and ch 3 more. Starting in the fourth ch from hk and following the chart for color changes, work 1 dc in each ch across, ch 2, and turn. Work even in dc on 62 sts (ch-2 counts as 1 dc) to completion of the chart. Fasten off.

Rectangle No. 2: Make two: With MC, ch 61. Change to color A and ch 3 more. Starting in the fourth ch from hk and following the chart for color changes, work 1 dc in each ch across, ch 2, and turn. Work even on 62 sts to the completion of the chart. Fasten off.

Rectangle No. 3: Make two: With B, ch 64. Starting in the fourth ch from hk, work 1 dc in each dc across, ch 2, and turn. Work even in dc on 62 sts, working 3 more rows with B, 4 rows with MC, 4 rows with C, and 4 rows with A. Fasten off.

Finishing: Work 1 row of color-over-color sc along the short edges of each rectangle, working the same number of sts along each edge. With MC, join the pieces (see diagram for positioning) by working a row of sl st between the adjacent pieces as follows: With the pieces lying flat, insert hk from right to left in the back lp of the first edge st on the right-hand piece and then from right to left through the back lp of the first edge st on the left-hand piece, yo and draw through all sts and lps on hk. Rep this process for each consecutive pair of sts until the seam is completed. Work the remaining seams in the same manner. Finally, with MC, work 11 rows of sc around the entire piece, working 3 sts in each corner. Fasten off.

Color Key:

□ = MC

／ = A

• = B

✕ = C

Rectangle No. 1

Rectangle No. 2

Rectangle No. 1 (reversed)	**Rectangle No. 3**	**Rectangle No. 1**
	Granny Square	
Rectangle No. 2		**Rectangle No. 2**
	Granny Square	**Rectangle No. 1 (reversed)**
Rectangle No. 1	**Rectangle No. 3**	

Note: Foundation-chain edge of each rectangle is placed to the outside edge of joined piece. Be sure to match stripes on adjacent rectangles when seaming.

27
Ripples

Approximate finished size:
48 by 58 inches

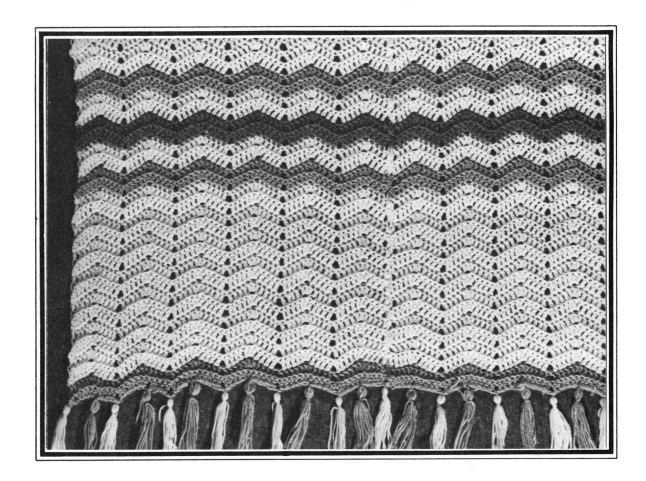

Three vertical strips of varying-width ripple waves, crocheted in the delicate shades of light rose, dusty rose, and mauve and set off by off-white, form this afghan. Once the strips have been seamed together, the piece is trimmed at each short edge with tassels of light rose and dusty rose.

Materials:
Knitting worsted:
    16 ounces in light rose (MC)
    8 ounces in dusty rose (A)
    12 ounces in off-white (B)
    4 ounces in mauve (C)
Aluminum crochet hook, Size I
Yarn-embroidery needle

Pattern Stitch:
Make a chain of the desired length.
Row 1: Ch 2, work 1 dc in the third ch from hk, 1 dc in each of the next 3 ch, * 3 dc in the next ch, 1 dc in each of the next 4 ch, skip 2 ch, 1 dc in each of the next 4 ch, rep from * across to within the last 5 sts, and end with 3 dc in the next ch, 1 dc in each of the last 4 ch, and turn.
Row 2: Working through only the back lps of the sts, ch 2, skip 1 dc, *1 dc in each of the next 4 dc, 3 dc in the next dc, 1 dc in each of the next 4 dc, skip 2 dc, rep from * across to within the last 5 sts, and end with 1 dc in each of the next 3 dc, skip 1 dc, 1 dc through both lps of last dc, and turn.
Repeat Row 2 for pattern.

Gauge in Pattern Stitch: 33 double crochet = 8 inches

Strips: Make three: With color A, ch 64. Then, working in pat st throughout, work in color pat of 2 rows A, 2 rows B, *10 rows MC, 2 rows B, 2 rows A, 2 rows B, 2 rows C, 2 rows B, 2 rows A, 2 rows B. Rep from * twice, ending with 10 rows MC, 2 rows B, and 2 rows A. Bind off.

Finishing: Sew the three finished strips together on the wrong side of the work, using an overcast st and matching the stripes.

Tassels: Make thirty-six in each of MC and color A: For each tassel, cut six 9-inch strands plus one 11-inch strand in the same color; cut one 6-inch strand in color A for both tassel colors. Tie the 6-inch strand around the center of the six 9-inch strands. Fold the strands in half and wrap the 11-inch strand twice around them ¼ inch down from the fold. Alternating colors, tie one tassel in each of the points of the two short edges of the afghan and in each of the indentations. Weave in the ends of the ties and trim the ends of the tassels evenly.

28
Granny
Goes
Free-Form

Approximate finished size:
  54 by 61 inches

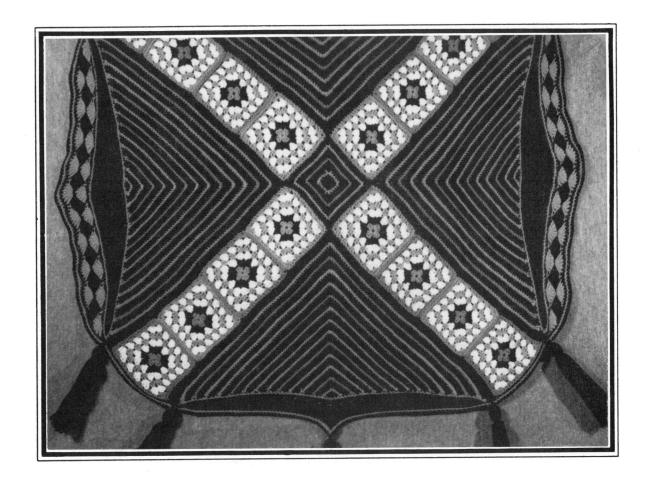

Sixteen traditional-style granny squares are placed in an X-formation to create the center of this piece, from which point the afghan is worked on in layers to create a symmetrical, free-form afghan. The colors used in the grannies are black, white, purple, cranberry, and jade, and the various borders are worked in purple and black. This afghan is suggested for experienced crocheters.

Materials:
Knitting worsted:
   28 ounces in black (MC)
   10 ounces in purple (A)
    7 ounces in cranberry (B)
    7 ounces in jade (C)
    4 ounces in off-white (D)
Aluminum crochet hook, Size I
Yarn-embroidery needle

Granny-Square Pattern: Ch 6 and join with sl st to form a ring.
Rnd 1: Ch 2, 2 dc in ring, (ch 1, 3 dc in ring) three times, ch 1, join with a sl st to the second ch of the starting ch-2. Fasten off.
Rnd 2: Attach the yarn in the first ch-1 sp, ch 2, (2 dc, ch 1, 3 dc) in the same ch-1 sp, *(3 dc, ch 1, 3 dc) in the next ch-1 sp (corner made), and rep from * twice more, joining with a sl st to the second ch of the starting ch-2. Fasten off.
Rnd 3: Attach yarn in the first ch-1 sp, ch 2, (2 dc, ch 1, 3 dc) in the same ch-1 sp, *3 dc between the next two 3-dc groups, one corner in the next ch-1 sp, and rep from * twice more, ending with 3 dc between the next two 3-dc groups. Join with a sl st to the second ch of the starting ch-2 and fasten off.
Rnds 4 through 6: Work as for Rnd 3, adding one more (3 dc between the next two 3-dc groups) between corners on each successive row.

Gauge: 3 double crochet = 1 inch

Granny Squares: Make four in each of the four following color pats.
Square No. 1: Starting ring and Rnd 1: A. *Rnd 2:* MC. *Rnd 3:* D. *Rnd 4:* C. *Rnd 5:* D. *Rnd 6:* A.
Square No. 2: Work as for Square No. 1 except work Rnd 6 with B.
Square No. 3: Work as for Square No. 1 except work Rnd 1 with B and Rnd 6 with A.
Square No. 4: Work as for Square No. 1 except work Rnd 1 with B and Rnd 6 with B.

Center Square: Make one: With MC, ch 6 and join with a sl st to make a ring.
Rnd 1: Continuing with MC, ch 2, work 11 dc in ring, and join with a sl st to the second ch of the starting ch-2. Fasten off.
Rnd 2: Working through only the back lps for the remainder of the square, attach A in the second ch of the starting ch-2 of the previous rnd, work 3 sc in the same ch (corner made), *work 1 sc in each of the next 2 sc, corner in the next sc, and rep from * twice more, ending with 1 sc in each of the next 2 dc; join with a sl st to the first st. Fasten off.
Rnd 3: Attach MC in the center sc of the first corner, ch 2, 2 dc in the

same sc, ch 1, 3 dc in the same sc, 1 dc in each of next 4 sc, (3 dc, ch 1, 3 dc) in the next sc st (corner made), and rep from * twice more, ending with 1 dc in each of the next 4 dc; join with a sl st to the second ch of the starting ch-2. Fasten off.

Rnd 4: Attach B in the first ch-1 corner sp and work 3 sc in the same sp, *1 sc in each of the next 10 dc, 3 sc in the next ch-1 sp (corner made), and rep from * twice more, ending with 1 sc in each of the next 10 dc; join with a sl st to the first st.

Rnd 5: Work as for Rnd 3 except work 1 dc in each of the 12 sc between corners.

Rnd 6: Work as for Rnd 4 with color C, working the corners as established and 1 sc in each dc between corners.

Rnd 7: Work as for Rnd 3, working the corners as established and 1 dc in each sc between corners.

Joining: Place the granny squares around the center square in an X-formation so that four squares radiate outward from each side. Place Square No. 1 closest to the center followed by Squares 2 through 4. When sewing, leave the two top lps of each st around the outside of each square free—sew on the wrong side of the work through the backs of the dc sts.

Triangles:

Row 1: Working in the angle formed by two adjacent sets of four squares, through the back lps only, with MC, and leaving the last lp of each dc on the hk, work (1 dc in each of the next 3 sts along the edge of the first granny square, yo, draw through all lps on hk—3 dc now worked tog). Now work 1 dc in each st along this side of the angle up to the last st on this side, skip this st and the first st on the second side of the angle, work 1 dc in each st along this side to the last 3 sts, and work the last 3 dc tog. Fasten off and return to the beg of the row.

Row 2: With A, (insert hk in st, yo and draw through) in each of the first 3 dc, yo and draw through all lps on hk (3 sc worked tog), work 1 sc in each st to the center of the angle, skip 2 center sts, work 1 sc in each st of the second side of the angle to the last 3 sc, and work the last 3 sc tog. Alternate Row 1 with Row 2 twelve times, working the dc rows in MC and each successive sc row in a color sequence of B, C, A to the end. Then work the last row with MC, working 3 dc tog on each side of the angle. Fasten off. Repeat to fill in the remaining three angles.

Border: *Side Edges:* Work along any two opposing edges (these will become the side edges) in the following manner, fastening off after each row, returning to the beg of the row each time, and working through the back lps unless otherwise specified.

Row 1: With A, work 1 row of sc along the outside edge of the completed, striped, angle portion, working 2 sc into the end of each dc row and 1 sc into the end of each sc row.

Row 2: With MC, work 1 row of sc, working the first and last 3 sc tog.

Row 3: With MC and starting in the first sc of the last row, work 1 sc in the first sc, *skip 2 sts, 3 dc in next st, and rep from * across, ending by skipping 2 sts and working 1 sc in the last sc.

Row 4: With MC, skip the first three clusters, fasten the yarn in the first dc of the next cluster, *3 dc between the next two clusters, and rep from * across to the last four clusters, skip the next cluster, and work 1 sc in the first dc of the next cluster.

Row 5: Fasten MC in the first st of Row 3, ch 2, and, keeping the last lp of each st on the hk, work 1 dc in each of the next 3 dc, yo, draw through all lps, work 1 dc in each st across, working 2 dc in each of the center 3 sts of row, and end 3 dc tog.

Row 6: With MC, work 1 row of sc around the entire border, starting from the beg of Row 1 and increasing 1 st in each of the center 3 sts.

Row 7: Rep Row 6 with color A.

Row 8: Rep Row 6 with MC.

Rep on the opposite edge of the afghan.

Border at Top and Bottom Edges: Work as for Rows 1 through 3 of the side edges. Then repeat Row 4 six times, skipping only one cluster at the beg and end of each row. Then work Rows 6 through 8.

Scalloped Borders at Top and Bottom Edges (Note: On these final borders, crochet loosely or with a larger hook so that the work will not pucker.)

Row 1: Attach color A in the first st of the last row worked, work 1 sc in the same st, *skip 3 sts, work 7 trc in the next st (scallop made), skip 3 sts, work 1 sc in the next st, rep from * across, adjusting the number of sts skipped if necessary so that there are eleven scallops across. Fasten off and return to the beg of the row.

Row 2: Attach MC in the fourth trc of the first scallop of the previous row, work 1 sc in each of the next 3 trc, 2 sc in the next trc, *1 scallop in the next sc, 1 sc in the fourth trc of the next scallop, rep from * across to the last scallop, ending 2 sc in the fourth trc of the last scallop of the previous row, 1 sc in each of the last 3 trc, and 1 sc in the last st of the row. Fasten off and return to the beg of the row.

Row 3: Attach A in the fourth trc of the first scallop of the previous row, *1 scallop in the next sc, 1 sc in the fourth trc of the next scallop, and rep from * across to the last scallop of the previous row (9 scallops). Fasten off and return to the beg of the row.

Row 4: Attach MC in the first st of Row 1 and work 1 row of sc through the back lps only along the entire scalloped border portion to the last st of Row 1. Fasten off and return to the beg of the row.

Row 5: With A, work as for Row 4.

Row 6: With MC, work as for Row 4.

Corner Edgings: On each exposed side of the four outer granny squares, work 1 row MC sc, 1 row A sc, and 1 row MC sc, fastening off at the end of each row and returning to the beg of row, while working through the back lps only.

Tassels: Make ten: For each tassel, cut fifty 21-inch strands of MC, one 6-inch strand, and one 23-inch strand. Tie the fifty strands in the center with the 6-inch strand, fold the tied strands in half, and wrap the center of the 23-inch strand twice around the outer strands 1½ inches below the fold. Trim the ends of the tassel evenly. Finally, tie one tassel in the center point of the two side edges and one tassel at both corners of the outside edge of each of the four outer granny squares.

29
Calico

Approximate finished size:
48 by 59 inches

Twenty raspberry-hued crocheted squares are embellished with gay white flowers. The squares are then joined vertically and horizontally with strips of crocheted white lace, and the whole finally edged with a white picot border.

Materials:
Knitting worsted:
   26 ounces in raspberry (MC)
   18 ounces in white (CC)
Aluminum crochet hooks, Sizes G and I
Yarn-embroidery needle

Pattern Stitch for Squares:
Row 1: Ch 1, 1 sc in the second ch from hk, 2 dc in the same ch, *skip 2 ch, (1 sc, 2 dc) in the next ch (shell made), and rep from * across, ending with 1 sc in the last ch, ch 1, and turn.
Row 2: *1 shell st in the next sc, skip 2 dc, and rep from * across, ending with 1 sc in the last sc, ch 1, and turn.
Rep Row 2 for pattern.

Pattern Stitch for Lace Strips:
Beginning at the narrow edge, ch 4.
Row 1: Work 2 dc in the fourth ch from hk, ch 2, 2 dc in same ch, ch 5, and turn.
Row 2: Skip 2 dc, (2 dc, ch 2, 2 dc) in ch-2 sp, ch 5, and turn.
Rep Row 2 for pattern until piece measures desired length. When the final row has been completed, *ch 5, 1 sc in the next ch-5 sp, and rep from * across one long edge, ending with ch 5 and 1 sc in the fourth ch of the foundation ch-4. Fasten off. Attach the yarn to the first turning ch on the opposite long edge, *ch 5, 1 sc in next ch-5 sp, and rep from * across. Fasten off.

Gauge: 1 pattern stitch = 1 inch for square pattern; 13 rows of lace strip = 9 inches on Size I hk (the strip should be 2 inches wide)

Squares: Make twenty: With MC and Size I hk, ch 28. Work even in pat st for 9 inches. Work 1 row of sc around the square, working 3 sc in each corner. Fasten off.

Lace Strips: With CC and Size I hk, make six strips that are 61 rows in length, three strips that are 77 rows in length, and two strips that are 83 rows in length.

Flowers: Make sixty: With CC and Size G hk, ch 4 and join with a sl st to form a ring. *Rnd 1:* *Ch 4; 2 trc in ring, ch 4, work 1 sl st in ring, and rep from * four times. Fasten off.

Finishing: Sew three flowers on each square, spacing them at random. Lay the squares out in a four-square-wide by five-square-long arrangement with spaces equal to the width of the lace between them. Sew the lace strips between the squares, thereby connecting the squares, sewing with CC through the finishing ch of the lace strip onto the edge of each square as follows: Sew the six 61-row lace strips across the four-square width of the afghan, placing one at the top and the bottom of the afghan and one of the remaining four between each horizontal.row of four squares, allowing 13 rows of lace along the edge of each 9-inch square with 3 rows of lace left free between each of the squares across. Now sew the three 77-row strips lengthwise between each row of four squares across, spacing them as before and laying them over the widthwise ones at the intersections. Last, sew the two 83-row strips to the long, outside edges of the afghan, again spacing as before but allowing both strips to extend 3 rows beyond the top and bottom squares on each side. Sew the strips together where they meet at each of the corners of the afghan.

Border: *Rnd 1:* With CC and I hk, work 1 row of sc around the edge of the piece, working 4 sc in each ch-5 sp and 1 sc in each sc. Join with a sl st to the first st. *Rnd 2:* *Work 1 sc in the next st, ch 5, work 1 sl st in the third ch from hk, ch 2, skip 2 sc, and rep from * around, ending by joining with a sl st to the first st. Fasten off.

30
Pinwheels

Approximate finished size:
54 by 54 inches

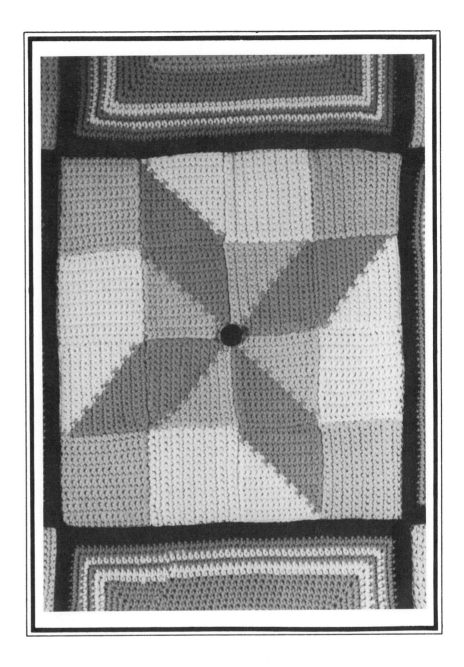

Five pinwheels are cleverly created of sixteen squares each, some pale yellow, some gold, some orange. When the crocheted piece is assembled into its final pieced-quilt-like pattern, the pinwheels are trimmed with dark brown centers and the piece is framed in dark brown.

Materials:
Knitting worsted:
  18 ounces in gold (A)
  12 ounces in pale yellow (B)
  12 ounces in orange (C)
   8 ounces in dark brown (D)
Aluminum crochet hook, Size I
Yarn-embroidery needle

Gauge: 7 stitches = 2 inches

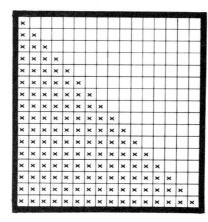

A/C Square Diagram
✕ = C
□ = A

Diagram No. 1

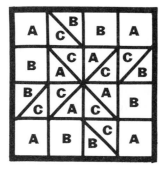

Pinwheel Squares: Make five: For each pinwheel square, make four of each of the following.
Color-A Squares: Ch 17. Starting in the second ch from hk, work 1 sc in each sc across, ch 1, and turn. Continue to work even in sc for 16 rows. Fasten off.
Color-B Squares: Work as for color-A squares.
Color-A/C Squares: Work in sc as for color-A squares, following the chart for color changes.
Color-B/C Squares: Work as for A/C squares, substituting color B for color A.

Large Contrasting Squares: Make four: With A, ch 27. Starting in the second ch from hk, work 1 sc in each ch across, ch 1, and turn. Continue to work even in sc on 26 sts for 34 rows. Then work 1 rnd of sc around the entire square, working 3 sc in each corner and joining with a sl st to the first st. Fasten off. Continue to work in rnds of sc as above, working 6 rnds C, 2 rnds B, 1 rnd A, 1 rnd B, 2 rnds A, and 2 rnds D. Fasten off.

Diagram No. 2

Pinwheels = P
Contrasting square = C

Finishing: Join the sixteen small squares for each of the five pinwheel squares, sewing on the wrong side of the work with a running back stitch and following Diagram 1 for arrangement. Following Diagram 2, sew the large contrasting squares and the pinwheel squares together, this time sewing with color D on the wrong side of the work with an overcast st. With D, work 1 row of sc around the entire joined piece, working 3 sc in each corner and joining with a sl st to the first st. Fasten off. With D, make a chain long enough to edge each joined pinwheel square and sew it in place along the inner edge of the D sc. * Finally, with D, ch 5 and join with a sl st to the first st to form a ring. Work 12 sc in the ring and join with a sl st to the first st. Fasten off. Sew this circle in the center of one pinwheel square. Repeat from * for each of the remaining four pinwheel squares.

Crocheted Lap Robes

31
Linked Chains

Approximate finished size:
40 by 54 inches

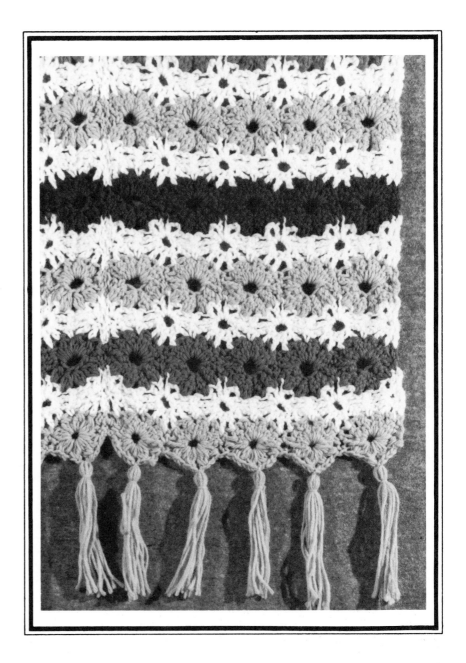

Jewel tones of aquamarine, ruby, and emerald are combined with white to form an interesting linked-chain design that resembles a chain of daisies. Crocheted in a simple-to-work but intricate-looking stitch, the afghan is composed of three strips joined, edged, and tasseled with aquamarine.

Materials:

Knitting worsted:
  12 ounces in aquamarine (MC)
  12 ounces in white (A)
  8 ounces in ruby (B)
  8 ounces in emerald (C)
Aluminum crochet hook, Size J
Yarn-embroidery needle

Pattern Stitch:

Make a chain of the desired length.

Row 1: Starting in the second ch from hk, work 1 sc, *skip 3 ch, (work 3 dc in the next ch, leaving the last 2 lps of each st on hk, yo and draw through all lps on the hk—cluster made), (ch 2, work 1 cluster in the same ch) three times, skip 3 ch, work 1 sc in the next ch, and rep from * across. Fasten off and return to the beg of the row.

Row 2: Attach yarn in the turning ch-1 at the beg of the previous row, ch 3, work 1 dc in the top of the first cluster of the previous row, 1 dc in next cluster, *ch 3, 1 sc in next ch-2 sp, ch 3, (1 dc in next cluster) four times, and rep from * across, ending ch 3, 1 sc in next ch-2 sp, ch 3, 1 dc in each of next 2 clusters, 1 dc in last sc, ch 1, and turn.

Row 3: Work 1 sc in the first dc, ch 1, skip 1 dc, 1 sc in the next dc, *ch 3, 1 sc in the next sc, ch 3, 1 sc in the next dc, ch 2, skip 2 dc, 1 sc in next dc, and rep from * across, ending ch 3, 1 sc in next sc, ch 3, 1 sc in next dc, ch 1, 1 sc in the third ch of the turning ch-3, ch 3, and turn.

Row 4: Work (1 dc, ch 2, 1 dc) in the first ch-1 sp, *ch 1, 1 sc in the next sc, ch 1, (1 dc, ch 2) three times in the next ch-2 sp, 1 dc in the same ch-2 sp, and rep from * across, ending ch 1, 1 sc in the next sc, ch 1, (1 dc, ch 2, 1 dc) in the last ch-1 sp, 1 dc in the last dc. Fasten off and return to beg of row.

Row 5: Attach yarn in the third ch of the starting ch-3 at the beg of Row 4, ch 1, 1 sc in same ch, *ch 3, (1 cluster in next dc) four times, ch 3, 1 sc in the next ch-2 sp, and rep from * across, ending ch 3, (1 cluster in the next dc) four times, ch 3, 1 sc in the last dc, ch 1, and turn.

Row 6: Work 1 sc in the first sc, *ch 3, 1 sc in the top of the next cluster, ch 2, skip 2 clusters, 1 sc in the top of the next cluster, ch 3, 1 sc in the next sc, and rep from * across, ending ch 1 and turn.

Row 7: Work 1 sc in the first sc, *(1 cluster, ch 2) three times in the next ch-2 sp, 1 cluster in the same ch-2 sp, 1 sc in the next sc, rep from * across. Fasten off and return to the beg of the row.

Repeat Rows 2 through 7 for pat.

Color Pattern:
Row 1: MC
Rows 2, 3, and 4: A
Rows 5, 6, and 7: B
Rows 8, 9, and 10: A
Rows 11, 12, and 13: MC
Rows 14, 15, and 16: A
Rows 17, 18, and 19: C
Rows 20, 21, and 22: A
Rows 23, 24, and 25: MC

Gauge in Pattern Stitch: 3 chain-link pats = 8 inches; 7 rows = 4 inches

Strips: Make three: With MC, ch 42 loosely and turn. Starting in the second ch from the hk, work in pat st throughout, working Rows 1 through 25 of color pat twice and ending with Rows 2 to 13. Fasten off.

Finishing: With MC, work Row 7 of pat st along the foundation-ch edge of each strip, working each four-cluster group in the same ch as the cluster groups on Row 1 and each sc in the same ch as the sc sts on Row 1. Fasten off. Sew the strips tog with an overcast st on the wrong side, working color over color.

Tassels: Make thirty: For each tassel, cut eight 13-inch strands, one 15-inch strand, and one 6-inch strand, all in MC. Tie the 6-inch strand around the middle of the eight 13-inch strands. Fold the strands in half and wrap the center of the 15-inch strand twice around the tied strands ¾ inch down from the fold. Tie one completed tassel in the center ch-2 sp of each pat st along both short edges of the afghan, weave in the ends of the ties, and trim the ends of the tassels.

32
The
Earthtone
Navajo

Approximate finished size:
  40 by 48 inches

Horizontal, repeating strips of authentic Navajo designs, single-crocheted in terra-cotta, taupe, sand, black, and off-white, are joined and edged with a black fringe at the ends.

Materials:
Knitting worsted:
   16 ounces in sand
   12 ounces in taupe
    4 ounces in black
    4 ounces in terra-cotta
    4 ounces in off-white
Aluminum crochet hook, Size J
Yarn-embroidery needle

Gauge: 8 stitches = 3 inches

Stripe Pattern: 2 rows black, 6 rows taupe, 2 rows black

Strips: For each, ch 105. Starting in the second ch from hk, work even in sc on 104 sts, working color pats as specified on the chart for each strip. (Note: When working with two colors on one row, work the sc over the thread not in use. On the rows where three colors are used, the unused yarn must be cut and the ends woven in later, as it is advisable to carry only one strand of yarn under the working color at a time.)
Strip No. 1: Make two: Work the stripe pattern and then work the chart for Strip No. 1 to completion; fasten off.
Strip No. 2: Make two: Work the stripe pattern and then work the chart for Strip No. 2 to completion; fasten off.
Strip No. 3: Make one: Work the stripe pattern and then work the chart for Strip No. 3 to completion. Finish by working the stripe pattern once more. Fasten off.

Finishing: With black, sew the strips together on the wrong side with an overcast st, placing the No. 3 strip in the center, a No. 2 strip on each side, and a No. 1 strip against each No. 2 strip, arranging them so that the unstriped edges face the center strip. Work 1 row of color-over-color sc along each long edge of the piece.

Fringing: Using 20-inch strands of black yarn, knot three strands in every other st along each short edge.

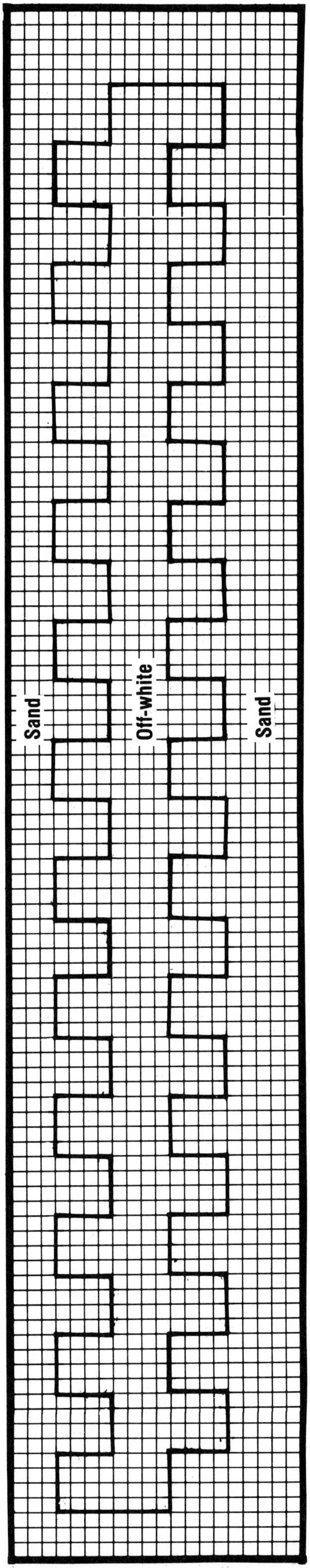

Strip No. 1

Sand

Off-white

Sand

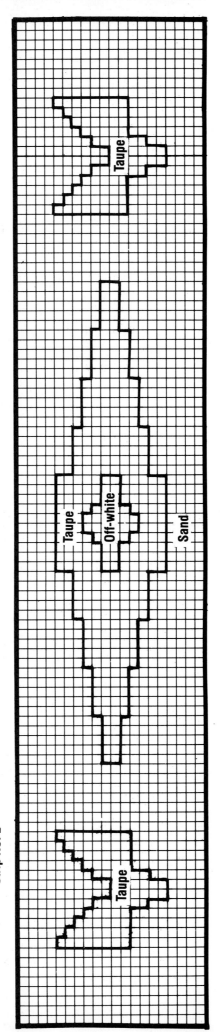

Strip No. 2

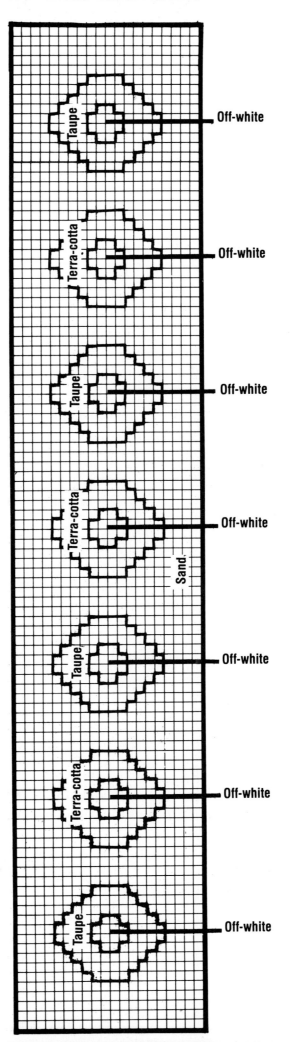

Strip No. 3

Off-white

Taupe

Off-white

Terra-cotta

Off-white

Taupe

Off-white

Terra-cotta

Sand.

Off-white

Taupe

Off-white

Terra-cotta

Off-white

Taupe

33
Bright
Geometric

Approximate finished size:
  37 by 51 inches excluding fringe

A square, two triangles, and four trapezoids crocheted of coral and charcoal are pieced together to form this interesting geometric lap robe. It is then framed by stripes of coral and charcoal and a luxuriant 6-inch-long fringe of charcoal. Because of its unique construction, this piece is recommended for experienced crocheters.

Materials:
Knitting worsted:
    28 ounces in charcoal (MC)
    16 ounces in coral (CC)
Aluminum crochet hook, Size I
Yarn-embroidery needle

Pattern Stitch:
Make a chain of the desired length.
Row 1: Work 1 sc in the second ch from hk, *1 dc in the next ch, 1 sc in the next ch, and rep from * across, chaining 1 if the row ends with 1 dc or chaining 2 if the row ends with 1 sc; turn.
Row 2: Work 1 dc in each sc and 1 sc in each dc, ending by chaining 1 if the row ends with 1 dc or by chaining 2 if the row ends with 1 sc.
Repeat Row 2 for pattern.

Gauge in Pattern Stitch: 3 stitches = 1 inch

Center Square: With CC, ch 4 and join with a sl st to form a ring.
Rnd 1: Work *(1 sc, 1 dc) in the center of the ring, rep from * three times, and join with a sl st to the first sc.
Rnd 2: Ch 2 and then work (1 sc, 1 dc) in the first sc, *1 sc in the next dc, (1 dc, 1 sc, 1 dc) in the next sc (corner made), rep from * twice, and end with 1 sc in the next dc; join with a sl st to the first dc of the rnd.
Rnd 3: Work 1 sl st in the next sc, ch 2, (1 sc, 1 dc in the same sc), and then *work along the next side of the square, working 1 sc in each dc and 1 dc in each sc as far as the center sc of the next corner. Work a corner in that sc, continue from * to the end of the rnd, and join with a sl st to the first dc of the rnd.
Repeat Rnd 3 to complete the square, working 2 more rnds in CC and then working (6 rnds MC, 6 rnds CC) twice. Fasten off.

Corner Shaping: *First Corner:* Using MC in pat st, beginning in the second dc of any corner st of the completed square, and working towards the next corner to the left, work 1 st in each st along this side of the square for 50 sts. Change to CC and work the remaining 7 sts on this side of the square in pat. Working with CC on only those 7 CC sts as established on the first row (these 7 sts will be decreased off after the seventh row), continue in pat st, decreasing 1 st at the beg and end of each row until 1 st remains. Fasten off. *Second Corner:* Work along the next side of the center square to the left of the side just worked as for the first corner, but on the first row, establish the first 7 sts in CC and the remaining 50 sts in MC. *Third Corner:* Work along the next side of the center square to the left of the side just worked as for the first corner. *Fourth Corner:* Work along the remaining side as for the second corner.

Trapezoids: Make two: With MC, ch 19. Change to CC, ch 9 more, and turn. *Row 1:* Starting in the second ch from hk and working in pat st throughout, work the first 8 sts in CC. Change to MC and work across the remaining sts. *Row 2:* With MC, work across to the last 7 sts of row, change to CC, and work across the remaining sts, increasing 1 st in the last st. *Row 3:* With CC, inc 1 st in the first st and work across the next 6 sts, change to MC, and work across the remaining sts. Repeat Rows 2 and 3 until there are 42 sts. Fasten off.

Reverse Trapezoids: Make two: Work as for the trapezoids above, making the following changes: With CC, ch 8. Change to MC, ch 20 more, and turn. Starting in the second ch from the hk, work the first 19 sts in MC. Change to CC and work across the remaining sts. Now, increasing on only the CC edge of the piece, shape the diagonal CC stripe as on the trapezoid above.

Triangles: Make two: With MC, ch 26. Starting in the second ch from hk, work 1 row even in pat. Now, dec 1 st at the beg of each row until 1 st remains. Fasten off.

Finishing: Block all pieces and then join them with an overcast st on the wrong side, matching the CC stripes on each of the four trapezoids to the coral stripes on the center square so that the stripes continue, as shown in the photo. Then sew one of the triangles in the opening between two of the trapezoids. Insert the remaining triangle in the same manner between the two trapezoids at the other end of the piece. Finally, work 6 rnds of CC and then 6 rnds of MC in pat st around the entire piece, working the corners as on the center square.

Fringing: Using 13-inch strands of MC, knot three in every other stitch around the afghan.

Crocheted Crib Blankets

34
Bow-Knot Gingham

Approximate finished size:
37 by 37 inches including edging

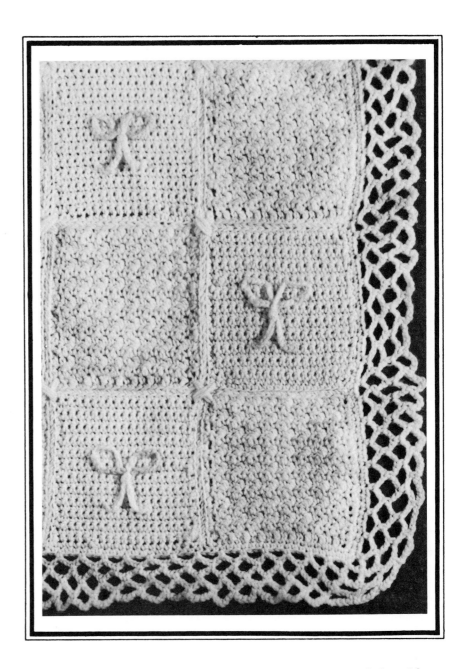

For this afghan, small, crocheted squares are joined in a ginghamlike pattern, appliquéd with tiny bow-knots, and edged all around with a lacy, chain-loop border. Ours is made in white, pastel pink, and a variegated yarn that blends with the two colors. If you're making one for a little boy, you might like to substitute a baby blue for the pink.

Materials:

Knitting worsted:

    4 ounces in white (A)

    4 ounces in baby pink (B)

    12 ounces in a yarn variegated in pink, white, yellow, and green (C)

Aluminum crochet hook, Size I

Yarn-embroidery needle

Pattern Stitches:

Make a chain of the desired length.

Pattern Stitch No. 1:

Row 1: Work 1 sc in the second ch from hk, *1 dc in the next ch, 1 sc in the next ch, and rep from * across the row, ending with 1 dc in the last ch, ch 1, and turn.

Row 2: Work 1 sc in the first dc, *1 dc in the next sc, 1 sc in the next dc, and rep from * across the row, ending with 1 dc in the last sc, ch 1, and turn.

Continue in this manner, working 1 sc in each dc and 1 dc in each sc on each row, chaining 1 st to turn when the first st is a sc and 2 sts when the first is a dc.

Pattern Stitch No. 2:

Row 1: Work 1 sc in the second ch from hk and 1 sc in each ch across the row, ch 1, and turn.

Row 2: Work 1 sc in each st across the row, ch 1, and turn.

Repeat Row 2 for Pattern Stitch No. 2.

Gauge in Pattern Stitches: 3 stitches = 1 inch

Squares: Make thirteen in color C with pat st No. 1 and six each in color A and in color B with pat st No. 2: Ch 19. Work even on 18 sts in pat until piece measures 6 inches. Fasten off.

Finishing: Work 1 row of color-over-color sc around each square, working 3 sc in each corner. Following the chart, join the pieces with an overcast st on the wrong side.

Bow Knots: Make twelve: With color C, ch 70 and fasten off. Tie each chain into a bow, and sew one to the center of each color-A and color-B square, as shown. With four strands of C, embroider a cross-stitch to cover each point of joining of the squares.

Edging: Join color C in any sc stitch on the edge of the blanket and work 1 row of sc around the outer edge, working 3 sts in each corner. Join with a sl st to the first st and then work as follows:

Rnd 1: *Ch 5, skip 2 sts, sc in the next st, and rep from * around (skipping just 1 sc at each corner point of turning), ending with a sl st in the first st.

Rnd 2: Sl st in the first and second ch of the next ch-5 lp, work 1 sc in the next ch, *ch 5, work 1 sc in the third ch of the next ch-5 lp, and rep from * around, joining with a sl st in the first sc on this rnd.

Rep Rnd 2 twice and fasten off.

C	A	C	A	C
B	C	B	C	B
C	A	C	A	C
B	C	B	C	B
C	A	C	A	C

35
Woolly
Friends

Approximate finished size:
32 by 41 inches

In this afghan, alternating crocheted squares of mint green and white are joined with bands of white, woolly "fur" to match the coats of appealing little white lambs appliquéd onto the blanket.

Materials:

Knitting worsted:
   16 ounces in white (A)
   12 ounces in mint green (B)
   2 ounces in charcoal (C)
   Small amount in black (D)
Aluminum crochet hooks, Sizes G and I
Yarn-embroidery needle

Loop-Stitch Pattern:

Make a chain of the desired length.
Row 1 (right side): Work 1 sc in the third ch from hk, 1 sc in each ch across the row, ch 1, and turn.
Row 2: Skip the first sc, *insert hk in the next sc, and wind the yarn over the index finger. Holding the yarn 1½ inches above the work, yo and draw through (pulling the yarn from under the index finger). Drop the lp on the right side of the work, yo and draw through 2 lps on the hk, and rep from * across the row, ending with 1 sc in the turning ch of the previous row, ch 1, and turn.
Row 3: Work 1 sc in each st across the row, ch 1, being sure to work a sc over the st skipped at the beg of Row 2, and turn.
Repeat Rows 2 and 3 for pattern.

Gauge: On Size I hk: 3 stitches = 1 inch

Squares: Make six in color A and six in color B: With Size I hk, ch 28. Work even in sc on 27 sts for 9 inches. Then, continuing around the outer edge, work 1 row of sc around, working 3 sts in each corner as you turn. Fasten off.

Woolly Lambs: Make six: With Size G hk, work as follows:

Body: With A, ch 14. Work 6 rows in the lp-st pat. *Row 7:* Sl st in each st to within the last 5 sts, work 1 sc in each remaining st, ch 1, and turn. *Rows 8, 10, 12, and 14:* Work Row 2 of the lp-st pat, working in the remaining sc sts only. *Rows 9, 11, and 13:* Sl st in the first st and then work 1 sc in each of the remaining sts. Fasten off after Row 14.

Head: With C, ch 6. Then work even in sc on 5 sts for 2 rows. *Row 3:* Sl st in the first st, work 1 sc in each of the next 3 sts, sl st in the last st, and turn. *Row 4:* Skip the first sl st, sl st in the next st, work 3 hdc in the next st and a sl st in the next one. Fasten off.

Legs: Make four for each lamb: With C, ch 7 and then work in sc on 6 ch for 1 row. Fasten off.

Tail: With C, ch 3, turn, work 1 sl st in each ch, and fasten off.

Ear: With C, ch 3 and turn. Then skip the first ch, work 1 sl st in the next ch, 1 sc in the next, and fasten off.

Loop-Stitch Joining Strips: Make two: With Size I hk and color A, ch 190. Then work in the lp-st pat, working Rows 1 through 3 once and Rows 2 and 3 twice; fasten off.

Edging: With color A and Size I hk, work an edging around each square as follows:
Rnd 1: Work 1 row of sc around the outer edge, working 3 sc in each corner st as you turn. Then join the end of the rnd with a sl st to the first st.
Rnd 2: Ch 2, work 2 hdc in the first st of the ch-2, *skip 2 sts, work 3 hdc in the next st, and rep from * around, working 5 hdc in each corner and ending by skipping 2 sts and joining to the second st of the starting ch-2 with a sl st; fasten off.

Finishing: Sew the body, head, leg, tail, and ear pieces of each lamb onto each of the color-B squares, as shown in the photograph, embroidering on each head piece a small, black French-knot "eye". Then overcast the squares together on the wrong side in three strips of four squares each, two of which should be arranged in a color sequence of B, A, B, A and the third of which should be arranged A, B, A, B. Using the A, B, A, B strip as the center of the afghan, join the three strips, placing a long lp-st strip between each two panels.

36
Baby's Own

Approximate finished size:
  31 by 42 inches including edging

In preparation for baby's arrival, a rectangle measuring 21 by 32 inches and a 10-inch square are both crocheted with white yarn and then laid aside until the big day. At that time, the square is framed with an edging worked in either pink or blue and the baby's name and birthdate are "inscribed" on it with chains crocheted of the same color. The "birth announcement" is then sewn onto the rectangle, which is finished with a lacy, 5-inch-wide border.

Materials:

Knitting worsted:

    12 ounces in white (MC)

     8 ounces in baby pink or medium blue (CC)

Aluminum crochet hook, Size I

Yarn-embroidery needle

Pattern Stitch for Main Piece:

Make a chain of the desired length.

Row 1: Ch 1, work 1 sc in the second ch from hk, *skip 2 ch, 5 dc in next ch, skip 2 ch, 1 sc in the next ch, rep from * across, ch 3, and turn.

Row 2: Work 2 dc in the first sc, *skip 2 dc, 1 sc in the next dc, skip 2 dc, 5 dc in the next sc, rep from * across, ending skip 2 dc, 1 sc in the next dc, skip 2 dc, 3 dc in the last st, ch 1, and turn.

Row 3: Work 1 sc in the first dc, *skip 2 dc, 5 dc in the next sc, skip 2 dc, 1 sc in the next dc, rep from * across, and end by working 1 sc in the turning ch of the previous row, ch 3, and turn.

Repeat Rows 2 and 3 for pattern.

Pattern Stitch for Edging:

Beginning at the narrow edge, loosely ch 11.

Row 1: Work (3 dc, ch 2, 1 dc) in the seventh ch from the hk, *skip 1 ch, (3 dc, ch 2, 1 dc) in the next ch, rep from * once, ch 6, and turn.

Row 2: Work *(3 dc, ch 2, 1 dc) in the next ch-2 sp, rep from * twice more, ch 6, and turn.

Repeat Row 2 for pattern until piece measures desired length.

Gauge in Pattern Stitch: 3 stitches = 5 inches

Main Piece: With MC, ch 73. Then work even in pat until piece measures 32 inches. Fasten off.

Center Square: With MC, ch 36. Starting in the second ch from hk, work 1 sc in each ch across, ch 1, and turn. Continue to work in sc on 35 sts until the piece measures 10 inches. Fasten off.

Edging: With CC, work the edging st until the piece measures 32 inches.

To shape the corner: On the next row, work in pat across. At the end of the row, ch 2, work 1 sc in the ch-6 lp of the previous row, ch 3, and turn. *Next row:* Work across the row in pat, ending ch 6, and turn as usual. *Next row:* Work across the row, ending ch 2, 1 sc in the sc in the ch-6 lp of the first row of the corner shaping, ch 3, and turn. Rep from * twice to complete the corner shaping. Now, always working the corner shapings at the same inner edge of the border piece so that the border becomes a rectangular-shaped frame, work even in pat st for

21 inches more, work the corner shaping, work even for 32 inches, work the corner shaping, work even for 21 inches, work the corner shaping, and then work 2 rows even in pat, ending at the inner edge of the border piece with ch 5 instead of ch 6. Working back along the inner edge of the border and chaining loosely, work 1 sc in the next ch-3 sp of the corner shaping, ch 3, work 1 sc in the second of 4 sc at the inner corner edge, *ch 3, work 1 sc in the next ch-6 lp, rep from * to the next corner shaping, working it as for the first corner, and continue in this manner until the entire inside edge is completed. Fasten off.

Finishing:

With MC, work 1 row of sc around the main piece and the center square. Sew the edging around the main piece, stitching through the finishing chain on the inside of the edging. Sew the corner seam of the edging. With CC, make a chain long enough to edge the center square and sew it in place (see photo). With CC, make enough chains of the lengths necessary to shape into 1½-inch-tall letters and numbers to add the name and birthdate. Pin and then sew them in place, spacing each line of lettering over 6 rows of sc on the center square. With CC and a lazy daisy stitch (see Stitch Glossary), embroider a small flower in the upper right-hand and the lower left-hand corners of the square. Finally, center it on the main piece and sew it in place.

Stitch Glossary

FOR KNITTERS

Casting On

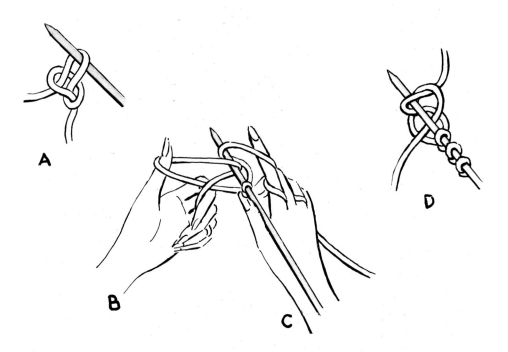

Make a slip loop on the needle, allowing 2 yards of yarn for every 100 stitches to be cast on, more if your yarn is heavier than average weight and less if it is lighter. This is your first stitch (A). Holding the needle in your right hand with the short end of the yarn toward you, *(1) loop the short end around your left thumb and insert the needle from front to back through this loop (B), (2) wind the yarn attached to the ball under and around the needle (C), (3) draw the yarn through the loop and pull on the short end to tighten it (D). (4) Repeat from * for the number of stitches desired.

Knitting

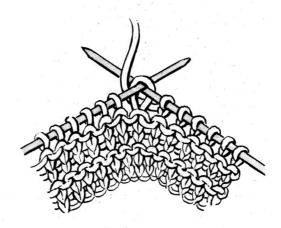

Holding the needle containing the cast-on stitches in your left hand with the yarn to the back of the work, *insert the right-hand needle from left to right through the front of the first stitch, wrap the yarn around the right-hand needle to form a loop, slip the needle and the loop through the stitch to the front, and slip the stitch just worked off the left-hand needle. This is your first knit stitch. Repeat from * in the same manner across all stitches on the left-hand needle.

Purling

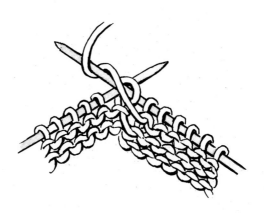

*Holding the yarn in front of the work, insert the right-hand needle from right to left through the front of the stitch on the left-hand needle, wrap the yarn completely around the right-hand needle, forming a loop, slip the needle and the loop through the stitch towards the back, and slip the stitch just worked off the left-hand needle. Repeat from * until all stitches are worked.

Binding Off

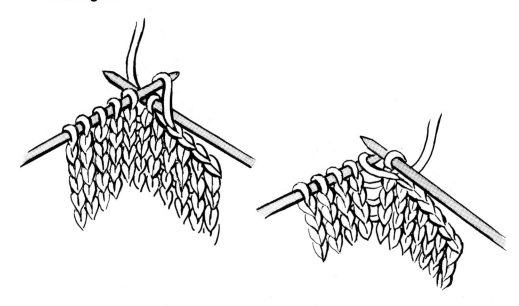

Knit the first 2 stitches. Then *insert the point of the left-hand needle into the first stitch on the right-hand needle, lift this stitch over the second stitch, and drop it off needle. Knit another stitch and repeat from * across the number of stitches to be bound off. When all the stitches are to be bound off at the end of a piece of work, complete the remaining stitch by breaking off the yarn and drawing it through the stitch.

Increasing

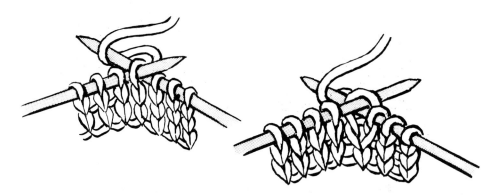

Insert the right-hand needle from right to left through the back of the next stitch on the left-hand needle, wrap the yarn around the needle to form a loop, slip the needle and the loop through to the front, forming a new stitch on the right-hand needle, and then knit the same stitch on the left-hand needle in the usual manner.

150

Decreasing

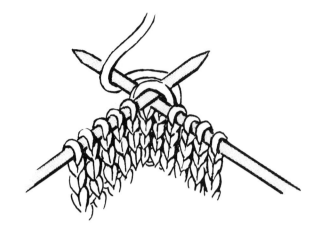

Insert the right-hand needle through two stitches on the left-hand needle and work them together as one stitch.

Slip Stitch

Insert the right-hand needle from right to left through the front of the stitch to be slipped and transfer it onto the right-hand needle without changing the position of the yarn.

Pass Slip Stitch Over

Lift the slipped stitch with the point of the left-hand needle, pass it over the next one or two stitches, as specified, and drop it from the left-hand needle.

Ripping Out

To rip out, withdraw your needle, unravel the yarn to one row below where an error occurred, and then rip out the next row stitch by stitch, inserting one of the two free needles into each stitch as you go. You are now ready to continue with your knitting.

FOR CROCHETERS

Foundation Chain

Knot a slip loop onto a hook. Holding the hook in your right hand, the end of the yarn extending from the loop in your left hand, and the main length of yarn over the index finger of your left hand, *place the main length over the hook. Then draw the yarn and the hook through the loop (first stitch). Repeat from * for the number of stitches desired. Turning chains are worked in the same way, as are chain stitches indicated in a pattern stitch, using the last loop worked as the first one through which your yarn and hook are drawn.

Slip Stitch

Insert a hook in the stitch, place the yarn over the hook, and draw it through the stitch and the loop on the hook.

Single Crochet

Insert a hook in the stitch, place the yarn over the hook and draw it through the stitch, yarn over the hook again and draw it through the two loops remaining on the hook.

Half Double Crochet

Place the yarn over the hook, insert the hook in the stitch, yarn over again and draw through the stitch, yarn over again and draw it through the three loops remaining on the hook.

Double Crochet

Place the yarn over the hook, insert the hook in the stitch, yarn over and draw it through the stitch, yarn over and draw it through two loops on the hook, yarn over and draw it through the two loops remaining on the hook.

Treble Crochet

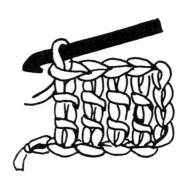

Place the yarn over the hook twice, insert a hook in the stitch, yarn over and draw through the stitch, (yarn over and draw through two loops on the hook) three times.

Increasing

Increasing involves the working of two stitches in the same stitch, thus forming an extra stitch. This is usually done by making the extra stitch in the same pattern as the original one in which the increase is being made and it can be worked at any point of the row, as well as at the beginning and end.

Decreasing

Decreasing when working with basic stitches involves the working of two stitches as one, thus decreasing, or "losing," one stitch. As in increasing, this can be worked with many stitches on any part of the row, as well as at the beginning and end. To decrease when using basic stitches on single crochet rows, draw up a loop in the next single crochet, draw up a loop in the following single crochet, wrap the yarn over the hook, and draw through all three loops at once. For double crochet, work the first double crochet to the point at which two loops remain on the hook, place the yarn over the hook, and insert the hook in the next stitch, yarn over and draw through the stitch, yarn over and draw through two loops, yarn over and draw through the remaining loops.

FOR EMBROIDERERS

French Knots

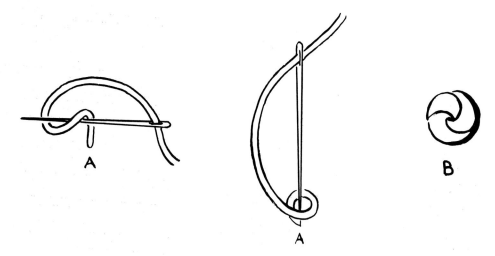

Bring the yarn through from the wrong to the right side at point (A), wrap it around the needle once or as many times as desired, and then pass the needle down through the fabric at point (A). The completed stitch should look like (B) above.

Stem Stitches

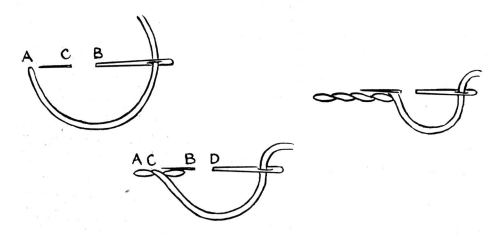

Bring the yarn through at point (A) on a traced or given line, pass the needle through the fabric from (B) to (C), and then pass the needle through from (D) to (B). Continue in this manner for the length desired.

Overcast Stitches

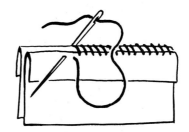

Bring the yarn through two thicknesses of fabric in one motion, as shown.

Running Chain Stitches

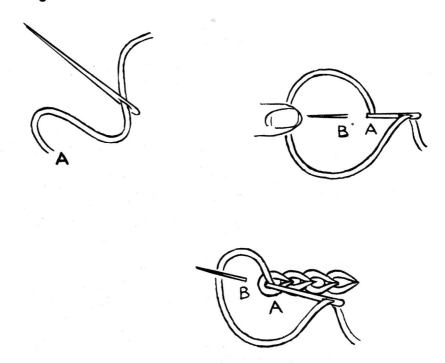

Work this stitch along a traced or other established line. Bring the yarn up through the line at any point to be marked (A), pass the needle through from (A) to (B), and then draw it through. Continue in this manner, passing the needle through from (A) to (B), for the length desired.

Satin Stitches

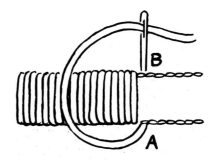

Bring the yarn through at (A) along any traced or other established line and pass the needle down through the fabric at (B) on another established line at the opposite side of the stitch. Then carry the needle across the back of the material and pass it through at the point next to (A). Continue to work in the same manner as for the first stitch.

Lazy Daisy Stitches

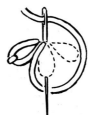 

Bring the yarn through at the base of the petal on a traced or given line. Then loop the yarn around the needle and pass the needle back through the fabric, bringing it up at the center top of the petal with the yarn under the needle. Make a small stitch over the loop to hold it in place, pass the needle through the fabric, and bring it up at the base of the next petal to be made.

Running Back Stitch

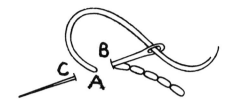

Working from right to left along a traced line, bring the yarn up through the traced line at (A), pass it through the fabric at (B), and bring it out at (C). Continue to work in this manner.

Cross-Stitch on Afghan Stitch

Each vertical bar of the afghan stitch counts as one stitch. Following the desired chart for embroidery design and working from left to right, join the yarn on the wrong side of the work in the small bottom space that occurs after the vertical bar. Bring the needle through to the right side, work across the next vertical bar into the top space occurring after that bar, and then draw the needle through the bottom hole directly below (A). When the necessary number of stitches have been worked in this manner, complete the stitch by forming a cross from right to left (B). To avoid puckering, do not pull too tightly.

Index